Civil Engineering

Practice Examination #1

Timothy J. Nelson, PE

Civil Engineering Practice Examination #1
Timothy J. Nelson

To report errors in this text, contact: tim@engineeringvideos.net

13-Digit ISBN: 9780615646220
10-Digit ISBN: 0615646220

EngineeringVideos.Net

Table of Contents

Introduction

Civil Engineering Practice Examination #1 provides 40 multiple-choice civil engineering exam problems to help civil engineers prepare for their professional licensing examinations.

Breadth Exam Topics

Civil Engineering Practice Examination #1 follows the specifications of the breadth examination (morning session), as defined by the National Council of Examiners for Engineering and Surveying (NCEES). This exam includes 8 questions from each of the 5 civil engineering sub-disciplines tested during the morning session of the Civil PE Exam:

- Water Resources and Environmental Engineering (8 questions)
- Geotechnical Engineering (8 questions)
- Structural Engineering (8 questions)
- Construction (8 questions)
- Transportation Engineering (8 questions)

The questions in this exam are mixed up and in no particular order; they are not grouped or identified by their sub-discipline. Within each sub-discipline, different topics and kinds of problems are presented. For example, water resources and environmental engineering problems may involve open channel flow, water quality, groundwater, pumps, hydraulics, etc.

Each problem in this exam provides four possible answers. For each problem there is only one correct answer. The calculated answer will be equal to, or closest to one of the four multiple choice answers provided.

Each problem is a separate and complete problem; the solution to one problem does not depend on the solution to a different problem. The problems can be solved in any order, all are quantitative, there are no 'word problems', and there are no trick problems. It is possible however, that more information will be provided than is necessary to solve the problem.

Practice examination problems in this text are not extremely hard or extremely easy; they are designed to be similar in nature and level of difficulty as the breadth portion of the Civil PE Exam.

How this Book is Organized

This book is divided into three sections: Problems, Detailed Solutions and Quick Solutions.

Problems: The Problems Section lists all 40 problems, three problems per page. All problems are multiple choice.

Detailed Solutions: The Detailed Solutions Section includes a restatement of the problem, followed by an analysis showing one way to determine the correct answer.

Quick Solutions: The Quick Solutions Section only includes the letter corresponding to the correct answer (A, B, C or D).

Problem Layout

Each problem is divided into 4 parts: Find, Given, Analysis, and Answer.

Find: The parameter to be determined/calculated is identified and labeled.

Given: The variables are identified and labeled; usually a figure is provided. Four possible answers are given.

Analysis: The problem is solved. Equations, figures and tables are positioned on the left side of the page, while notes and commentary are positioned on the right side of the page. The analysis concludes by identifying the value of the parameter to be determined/calculated.

Answer: The letter (A, B, C or D) corresponding to the correct answer.

How to Use this Exam

Civil Engineering Practice Examination #1 should be used as an assessment tool for the test-taker to evaluate his or her strengths and weaknesses within the field of civil engineering.

Although the Detailed Solutions section explains the equations and process used to solve each problem, this practice examination does not teach the topics of civil engineering from scratch.

Notation and Terminology

Equations and inequalities are labeled and numbered using the notations shown below. Relationships involving 'at least' (≥) and 'at most' (≤) are considered inequalities. Not all equations or inequalities are labeled.

equation = eq. #
inequality = ieq. #

Figures in this examination are not necessarily drawn to scale, especially when a scaled drawing in the problem statement would give away the solution. It is advisable to rely primarily on the numbers and labels to understand each problem and solution.

Typically 3 or 4 significant figures are maintained when the problem is solved in the 'Detailed Solutions' Section. For a multiple choice examination, greater precision is rarely necessary.

There may be more than one method to determine the correct answer. The method used to solve each problem in this text is not necessarily the only way to determine the solution.

About the Author

Tim Nelson works as a Civil Engineer and Web Developer in Sacramento, California. He earned his Bachelor's and Master's Degrees in Civil Engineering in 2005 and 2007, respectively. Tim passed the Civil PE Exam in the State of California, in 2009.

Afterwards, Tim built the website EngineeringVideos.Net and created hundreds of short video example problems covering the various sub-disciplines of Civil Engineering.

Civil Engineering Practice Examination #1 is an extension of Tim's effort to help others successfully prepare for and pass the NCEES Civil Engineering Licensing Examination.

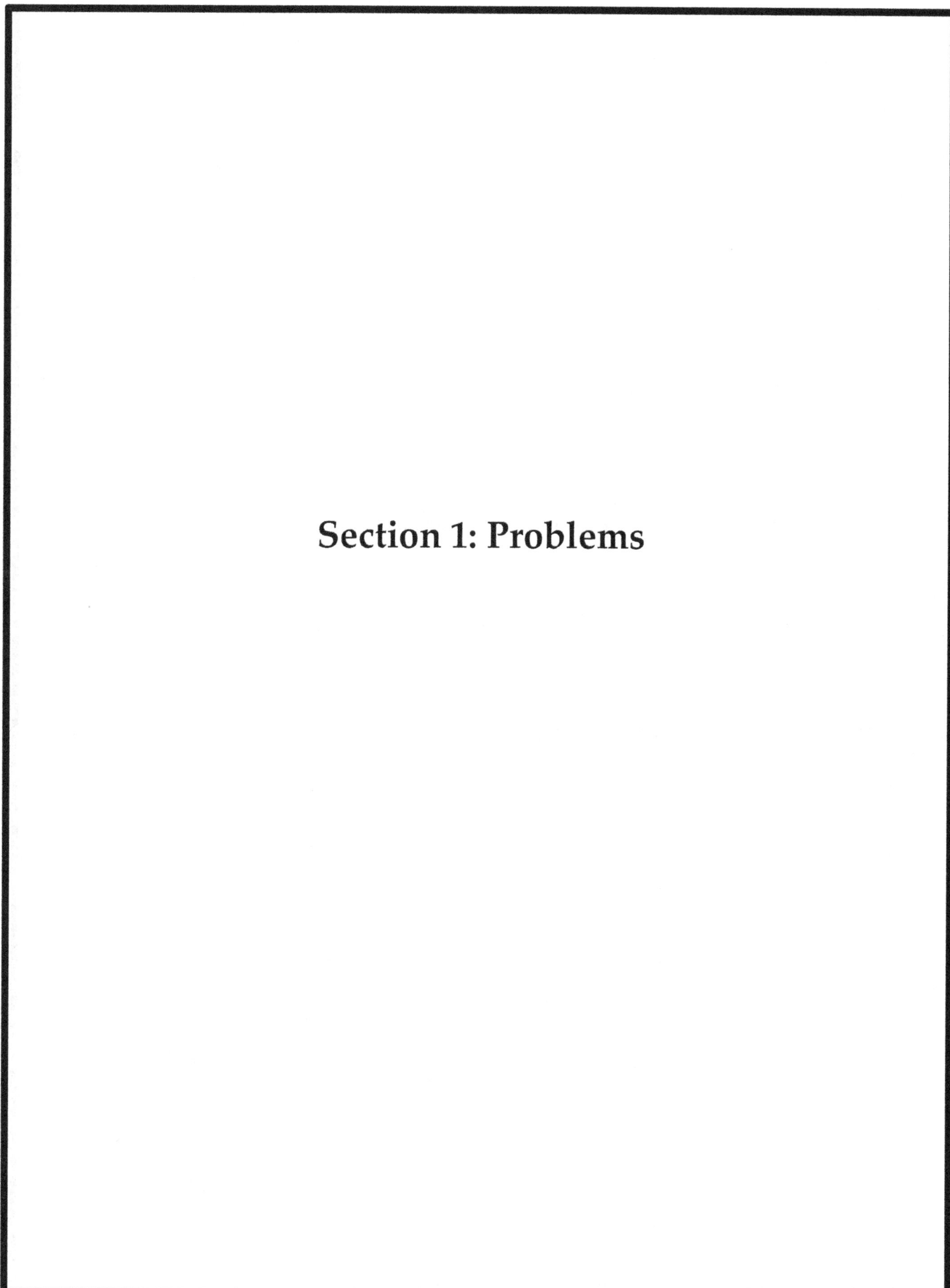

Section 1: Problems

(page intentionally left blank)

Problem #1

Find: F_{GF} ← the force in member GF

Given:

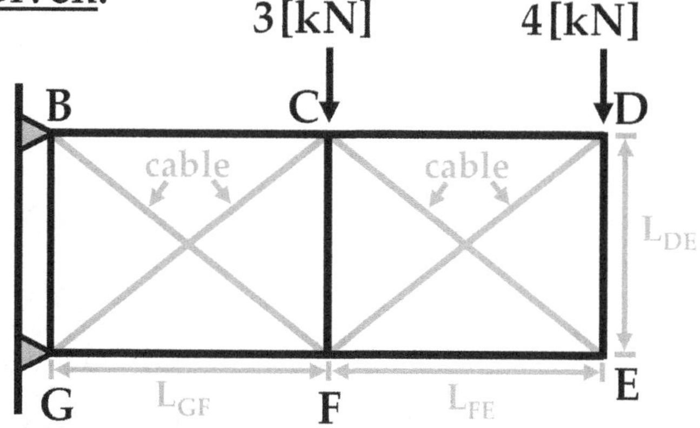

$L_{DE}=1.5\,[m]$
$L_{FE}=2.0\,[m]$
$L_{GF}=2.0\,[m]$
} length of members in the structure

$F_{GC}=0\,[kN]$ ← assume 0 force in cable GC

cables only sustain a tensile force

A) 0 [kN]
B) 11.67 [kN] (tension)
C) 12.33 [kN] (compression)
D) 14.67 [kN] (compression)

Problem #2

Find: w_{opt} ← the optimal water content

Given:

4 compaction tests were run on the same sample

laboratory test data

Test	W_W (weight of water)	W_S (weight of solid)	V_T (total volume)
A	0.97 [lb]	24.11 [lb]	0.244 [ft³]
B	1.18 [lb]	19.55 [lb]	0.193 [ft³]
C	1.79 [lb]	22.45 [lb]	0.228 [ft³]
D	1.84 [lb]	18.40 [lb]	0.206 [ft³]

A) 4%
B) 6%
C) 8%
D) 10%

Problem #3

Find: d ← the depth of flow in the channel

Given:

n=0.017 ← roughness coefficient

b=4 [m] ← base width

v=3.1 [m/s] ← channel velocity

S=0.001 ← channel slope

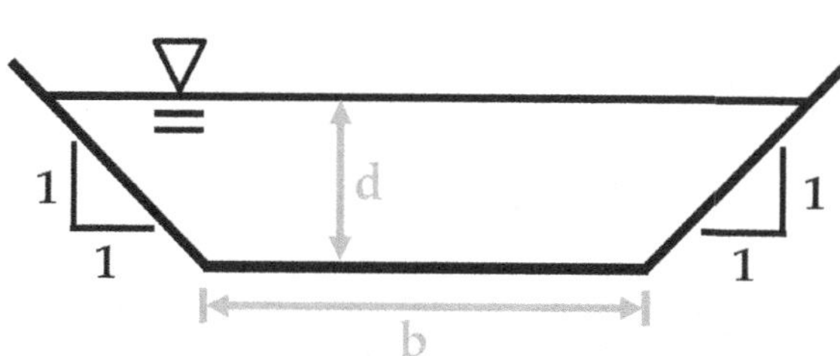

trapezoidal channel

the channel side slopes are 1:1

A) 1.2 [m]
B) 1.5 [m]
C) 1.8 [m]
D) 4.2 [m]

Problem #4

Find: A_1 ← the annual cash flow for years 1 through 17

Given:

A_2=$10,000 ← the annual cash flow for years 18, 19, 20 and 21

i=7.5% ← nominal interest rate (quarterly compounding)

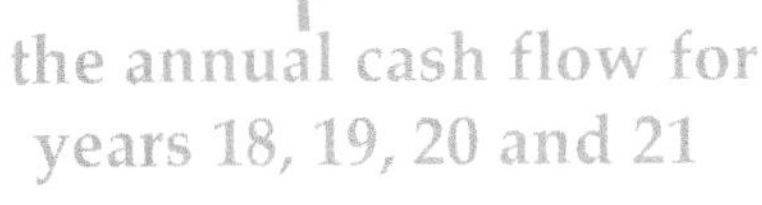

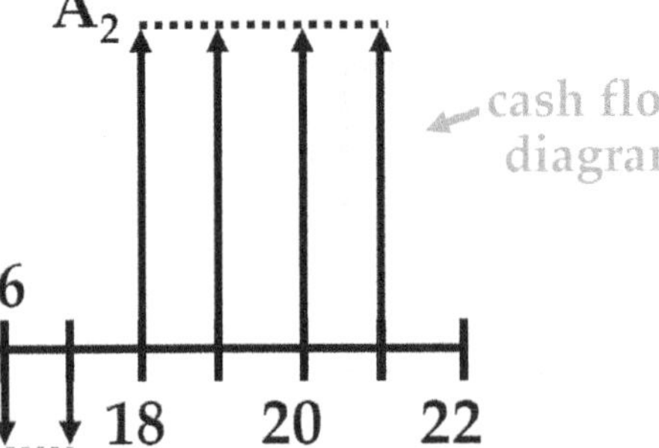

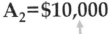

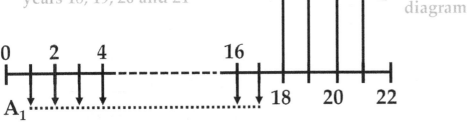

A) $1,000

B) $1,014

C) $1,038

D) $1,054

Problem #5

Find: $M_{x=5[m]}$ ← the moment at the mid-span of the beam

Given:

$P_A=P_C=8[kN]$ ← load at points A and E

$L_{AB}=2[m]$
$L_{AC}=3[m]$
$L_{CE}=7[m]$
$L_{DE}=2[m]$
} length between two specified points along the beam

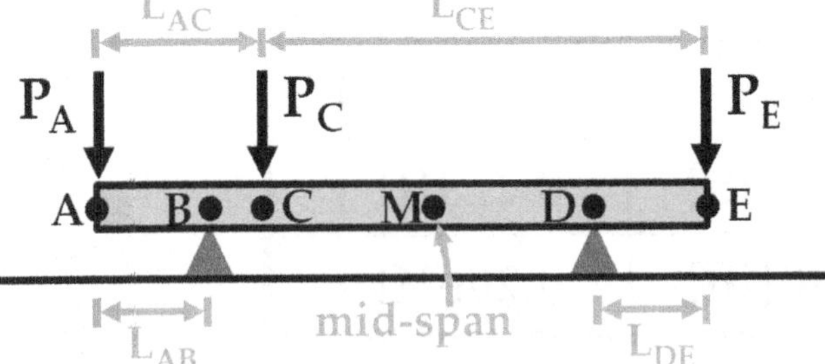

$P_E=20[kN]$ ← load at point E

A) 16[kN*m]

B) -13[kN*m]

C) -16[kN*m]

D) -24[kN*m]

Problem #6

Find: STA_B ← the stationing at point B

Given: STA_A=4+50 ← the stationing at point A

$I=28.5^{o}$ ← interior angle

L_{AC}=58.0[ft] ← distance between points A and C

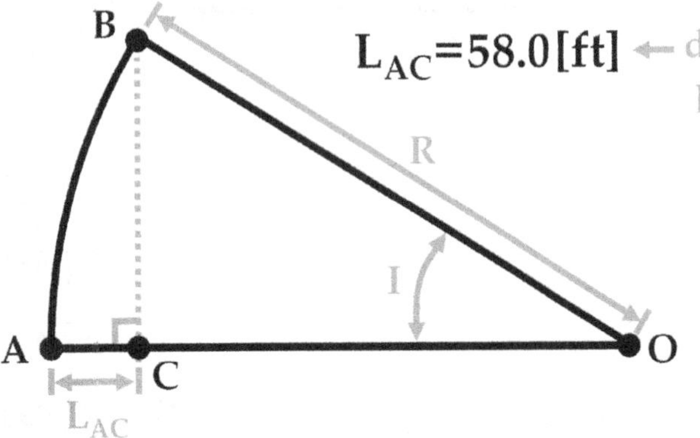

points A and B are connected by a horizontal curve.

A) 4+79

B) 5+05

C) 6+53

D) 6+88

Problem #7

Find: w_{clay} ← the water content of the clay layer

Given:

$d_{sand}=10[m]$ ← thickness of the sand layer

$d_{clay}=10[m]$ ← thickness of the clay layer

$\gamma_{T,clay}=18.15[kN/m^3]$ ← total unit weight of the clay layer

$SG_{clay}=2.65$ ← specific gravity of the clay layer

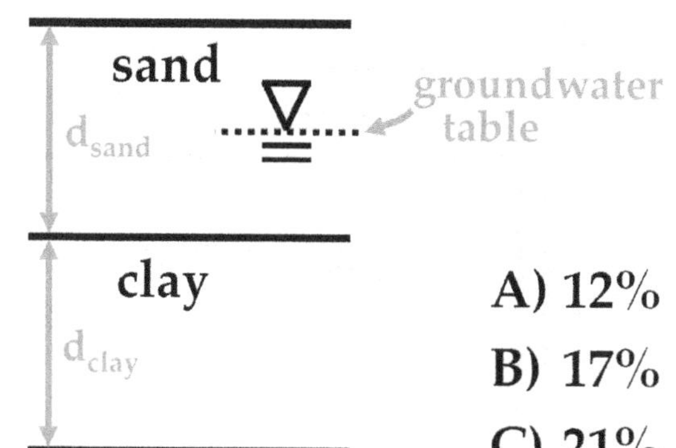

A) 12%
B) 17%
C) 21%
D) 35%

Problem #8

Find: LS_D ← the late start for activity D (permitting)

Given:

ID	Activity	Duration	Pred
A	Win Bid	0	-
B	Materials	3	A
C	Construction	7	B
D	Permitting	6	A
E	Inspection	2	C,D

$ES_A=1$ ← early start for activity A (win bid)

A) 3
B) 5
C) 7
D) 11

Problem #9

Find: $h_{f,AB}$ ← the headloss in the pipe between points A and B

Given:

$L_{AB}=150[ft]$ ← length of pipe AB

water flows through a smooth circular pipe

A → Q B

$Q=0.54[ft^3/s]$ ← flow rate

$v=2.75[ft/s]$ ← velocity

$T=68^{\circ}F$ ← temperature of water

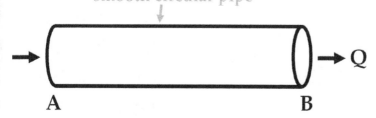

A) 0.06[ft]
B) 0.60[ft]
C) 6.00[ft]
D) 60.0[ft]

Problem #10

Find: r_2 ← the radius from the center of the well to point 2

Given:

$r_1=20[ft]$ ← distance from center of well to points 1 and 3
$r_3=100[ft]$

$s_1=4[ft]$ ← drawdown at radii 1, 2 and 3
$s_2=2[ft]$
$s_3=1[ft]$

$Y=150[ft]$ ← aquifer depth

$Q=30[gal/min]$ ← steady-state pumping rate

unconfined aquifer

A) 58[ft]
B) 66[ft]
C) 74[ft]
D) 82[ft]

Problem #11

Find: $Elev_D$ ← the elevation at point D

Given:

i	STA_i	$Elev_i$
A	10+00	243.0[ft]
B	12+00	239.0[ft]
C	STA_C	237.0[ft]
D	15+00	$Elev_D$
E	16+00	$Elev_E$

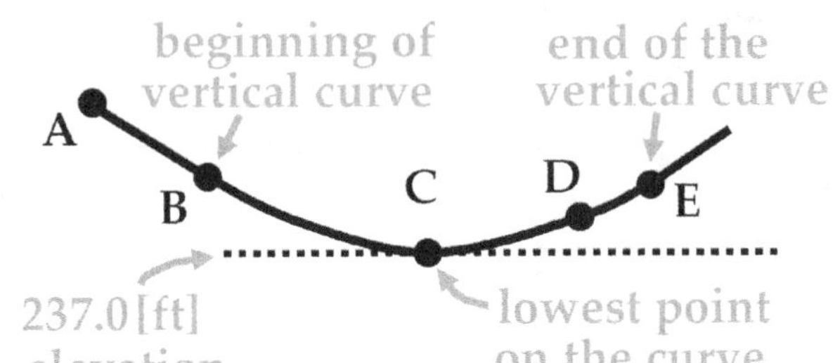

A) 237.5[ft]
B) 238.0[ft]
C) 238.5[ft]
D) 239.0[ft]

Problem #12

Find: V ← the volume of material

Given:

All side slopes are 2:1 (horizontal:vertical)

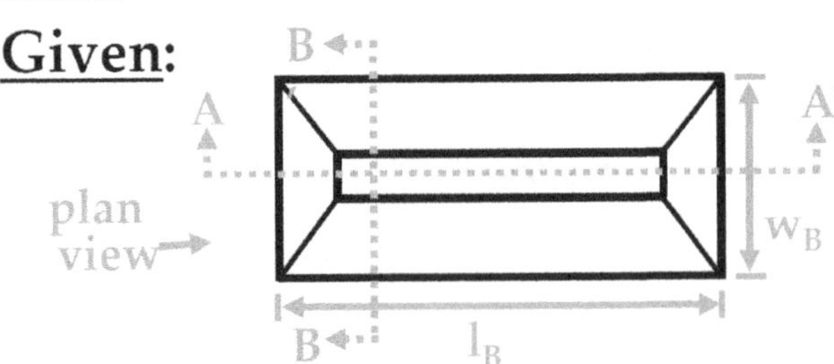

$l_B=120[ft]$ ← base length
$w_B=50[ft]$ ← base width
$h=10[ft]$ ← height

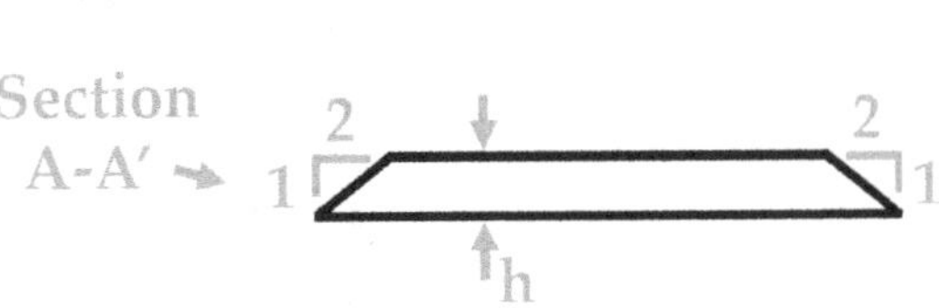

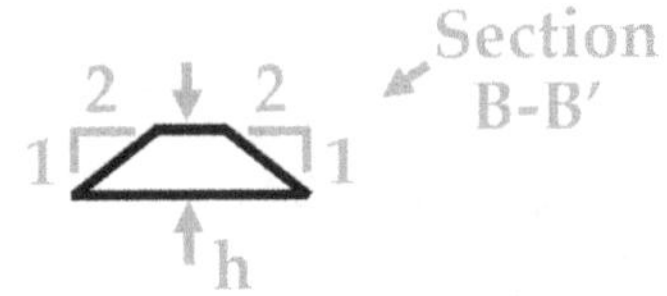

A) 1,160 $[yd^3]$
B) 1,260 $[yd^3]$
C) 31,000 $[yd^3]$
D) 34,000 $[yd^3]$

Problem #13

Find: g_B ← the grade of the curve at point B

Given:

g_1=1.75% ← approach grade

g_2=-0.75% ← departing grade

STA_A=12+50
STA_B=14+75
STA_C=18+50
} the stationing at points A, B and C

$Elev_A$=120.0[ft]
↑ elevation at point A

the crest vertical curve begins at point A and ends at point C

A) 0.4%
B) 0.6%
C) 0.8%
D) 1.0%

Problem #14

Find: Q_C ← the flow rate in stream C

Given:

T_B=20°C ← the temperature of stream B

Q_A=4.7[L/s] ← the flow rate in stream A

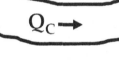

no chloride present in any stream

stream B is saturated in dissolved oxygen

DO_A=4.00[mg/L]
DO_C=5.00[mg/L]
} the concentration of dissolved oxygen in streams A and C

A) 2.87[L/s]
B) 5.83[L/s]
C) 6.41[L/s]
D) 7.89[L/s]

Problem #15

Find: L ← the length of the beam

Given:

E=2.9*10^7[lb/in^2] ← elastic modulus

I=200[in^4] ← area moment of inertia

y_{max}=0.17[in]
↑ maximum deflection in the beam

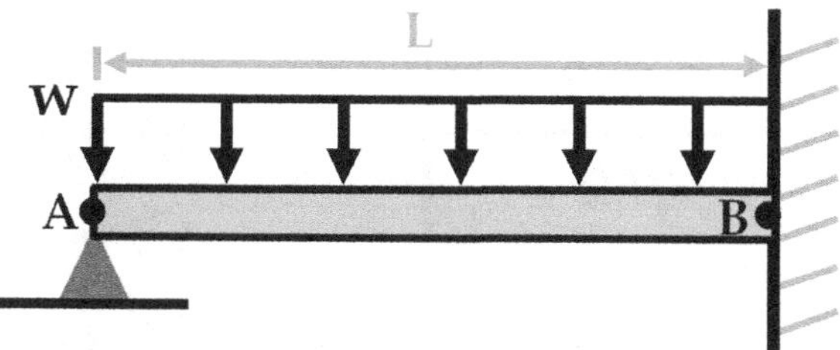

M_B=-40,500[lb*ft]
↑ moment in the beam at point B

← propped cantilever with uniform load

A) 9[ft]
B) 12[ft]
C) 15[ft]
D) 18[ft]

Problem #16

Find: P ← the axial force applied to the rod

Given:

$d_B=0.09[m]$, $d_S=0.05[m]$ } outer diameter of the brass and steel material

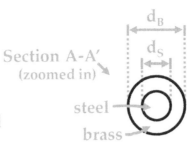

$E_B=1.05*10^{11}[N/m^2]$, $E_S=2.00*10^{11}[N/m^2]$ } elastic modulus of the brass and steel material

$L_o=0.644[m]$ ← initial length of rod

$\Delta L=0.002[m]$ ← change in rod length (elastic deformation)

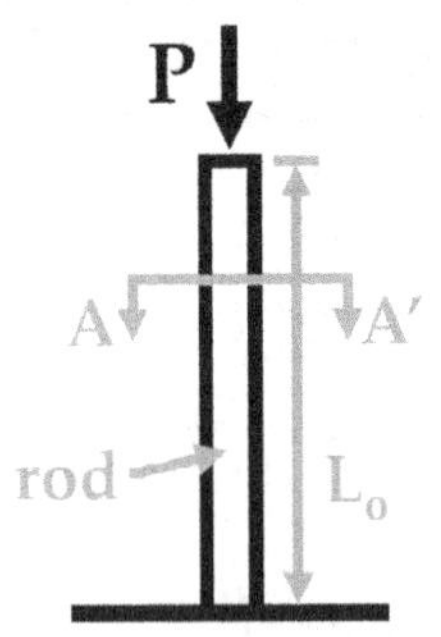

Section A-A′ (zoomed in): d_B, d_S, steel, brass

A) $1.96*10^6[N]$

B) $2.07*10^6[N]$

C) $2.65*10^6[N]$

D) $3.29*10^6[N]$

Problem #17

Find: G ← the grade of the road

Given: $v_i=100[km/hr]$ ← the initial velocity

$v_f=30[km/hr]$ ← the final velocity

$f=0.50$ ← the friction coefficient

$\Delta x=90[m]$ ← the distance the car travels while skidding from velocity v_i to velocity v_f

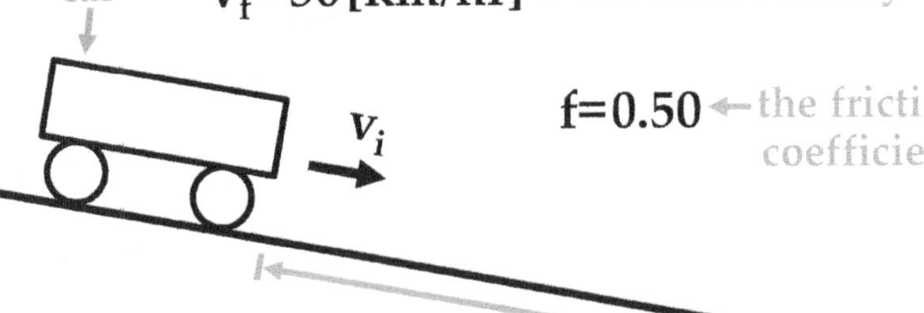

a negative grade refers to a downhill slope:

A) -0.04

B) -0.06

C) -0.08

D) -0.10

Problem #18

Find: Air Content ← the percent air content in the concrete mix

$\gamma_W=62.4[lb/ft^3]$ ← unit weight of water

Given:

Material	SG	Weight [lb]
Cement	3.15	658
Fine Aggregate	2.63	1,211
Coarse Aggregate	2.71	1,742
Water	1.00	260
Air	-	0

$V_T=27.00[ft^3]$ ← total volume of the concrete mix

A) 1.8%

B) 2.2%

C) 6.7%

D) 7.1%

Problem #19

Find: Soil Classification

Given:

Fine-grained soil

PL=37% ← plastic limit of the soil

liquid limit test data

Test	N (the number of drops)	w (water content)
A	18	60%
B	21	54%
C	35	35%

A) CL
B) CH
C) ML
D) MH

Problem #20

Find: L ← superelevation runoff

Given:

f_s=0.16 ← coefficient of static friction

SRR=1:300 ← transition rate

v=40[mi/hr] ← velocity

w=12[ft] ← lane width

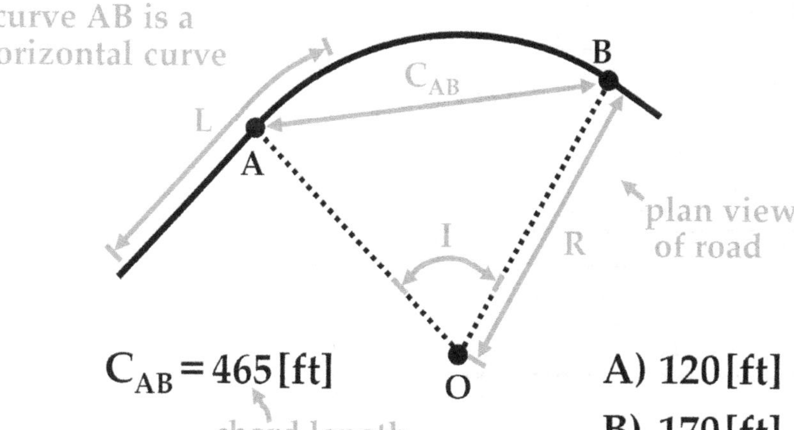

C_{AB}=465[ft] ← chord length

I=60° ← interior angle

A) 120[ft]
B) 170[ft]
C) 210[ft]
D) 250[ft]

Problem #21

Find: I ← the area moment of inertia about the x axis

Given:

h_f=2[in] ← the height of the flange

h_w=8[in] ← the height of the web

w_f=8[in] ← the width of the flange

w_w=2[in] ← the width of the web

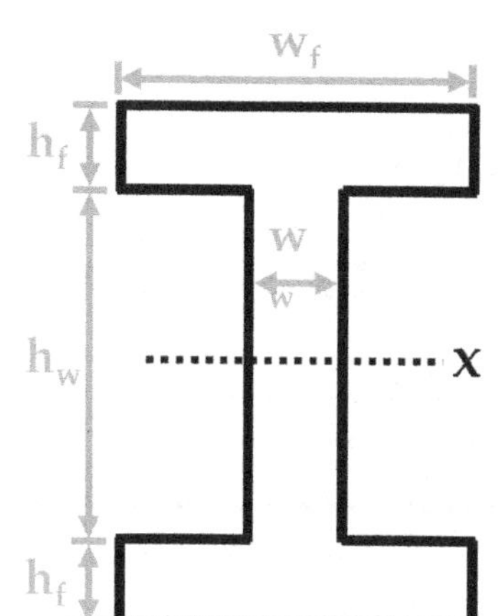

A) 405[in^4]
B) 490[in^4]
C) 810[in^4]
D) 890[in^4]

Problem #22

Find: W_{haul} ← the weight of extra soil needed to be hauled off site after the terrain is leveled to elevation=0[ft]

Given: w=30[ft] ← width of cut pile and fill pit (into and out of the page)

γ_T=120[lb/ft^3] ← the total unit weight of the soil

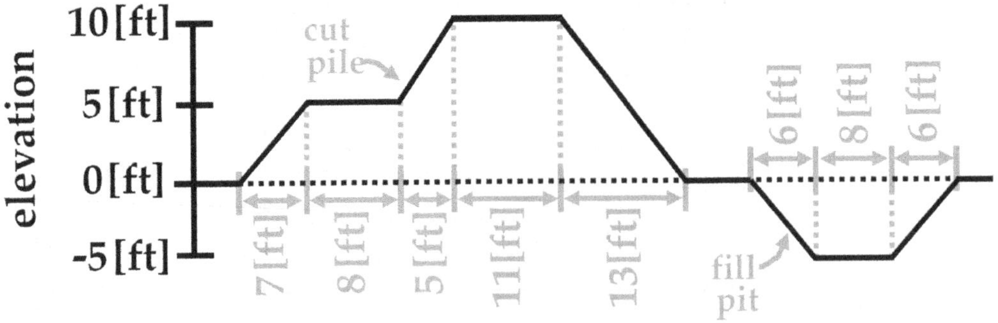

elevation: 10[ft], 5[ft], 0[ft], -5[ft]

cut pile; fill pit

7[ft], 8[ft], 5[ft], 11[ft], 13[ft]; 6[ft], 8[ft], 6[ft]

A) 120[ton]
B) 240[ton]
C) 360[ton]
D) 480[ton]

Problem #23

Find: σ_h @ d=12[ft] ← the horizontal stress at a depth of 12 feet

Given:

d_{gw}=4[ft] ← depth to the groundwater table

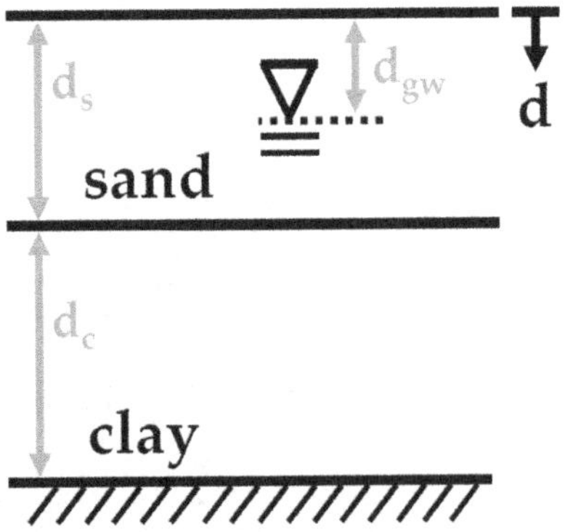

$K_{o,s}$=0.45, $K_{o,c}$=0.65 } at-rest lateral earth pressure coefficients for the sand and clay layers

d_s=8[ft], d_c=9[ft] } thickness of the sand and clay layers

$\gamma_{T,s}$=120[lb/ft^3], $\gamma_{T,c}$=100[lb/ft^3] } unit weights of the sand and clay layers

sand; clay; d_s; d_c; d_{gw}; d

A) 890[lb/ft^2]
B) 1,010[lb/ft^2]
C) 1,060[lb/ft^2]
D) 1,150[lb/ft^2]

Problem #24

Find: $y_{x=3[ft]}$ ← the deflection of the beam 3 feet from the end

Given:

E=2.9*10^7[lb/in^2] ← elastic modulus

I=6,000[in^4] ← area moment of inertia

k=3.3564*10^7[lb/ft] ← stiffness of the beam

P_B=4,000[k] ← point load at mid-span

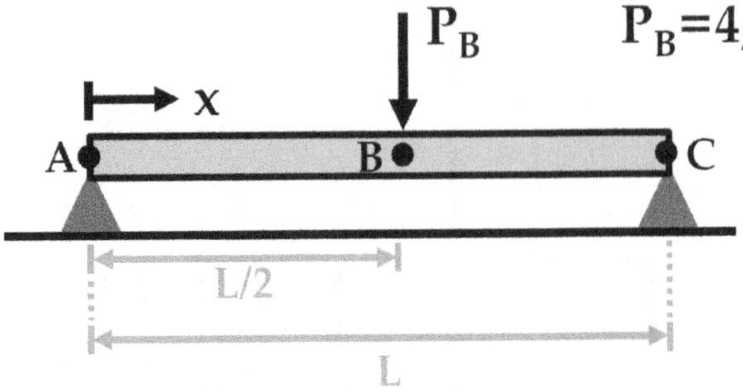

x; P_B; A; B; C; L/2; L

← simply supported beam with a point load P_B

A) 1[in]
B) 2[in]
C) 3[in]
D) 4[in]

Problem #25

Find: v_D ← the design speed of the curve

Given:

$R=500[ft]$ ← curve radius

$C=350[ft]$ ← chord length

the horizontal curve experiences no elevation change

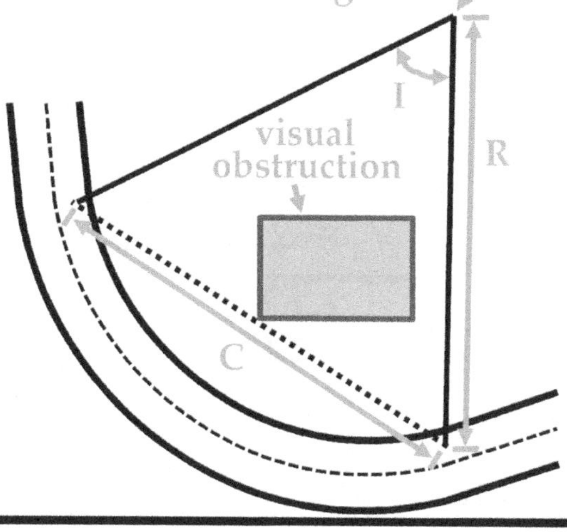

A) 40[mph]
B) 50[mph]
C) 60[mph]
D) 70[mph]

Problem #26

Find: C_{min} ← the minimum cost of plywood for concrete formwork

Given:

$t \leq 12[weeks]$ ← formwork must be completed in 12 weeks

$A_T=10{,}000[ft^2]$ ← total area of plywood required

$A_{use} \leq 1{,}000[ft^2/week]$ ← maximum weekly plywood use

Plywood Type	Cost per ft²	Uses
Standard	$2.25	3
High Density	$4.00	7

plywood may be reused each week up to either 3 or 7 total uses

A) $6,000
B) $6,250
C) $6,400
D) $6,650

Problem #27

Find: Q_B ← the flow rate through pipe B

Given:

$Q_A=14[gal/min]$ ← the flow rate through pipe A

$d_B=4[in]$ ← the diameter of pipe B

$d_C=6[in]$ ← the diameter of pipe C

$f_B=f_C=0.018$ ← the friction factor through pipes B and C

$L_B=L_C=40[ft]$ ← the length of pipes B and C

pipe schematic

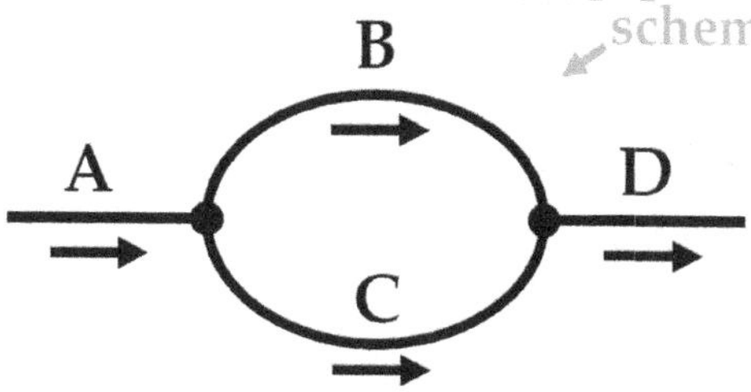

A) 3.7[gal/min]
B) 4.4[gal/min]
C) 5.0[gal/min]
D) 5.4[gal/min]

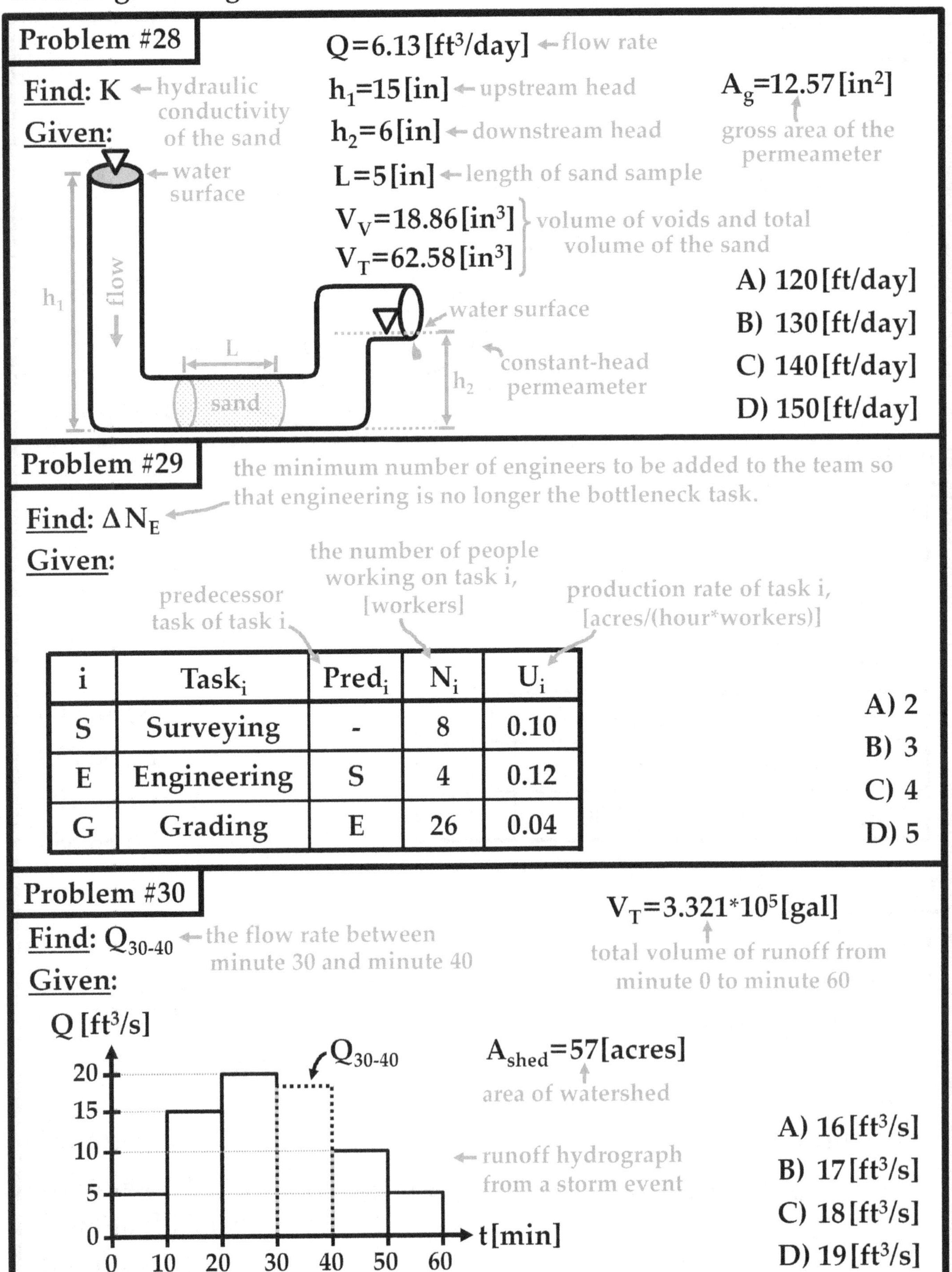

Problem #28

Find: K ← hydraulic conductivity of the sand

Given:

$Q=6.13[ft^3/day]$ ← flow rate

$h_1=15[in]$ ← upstream head

$h_2=6[in]$ ← downstream head

$L=5[in]$ ← length of sand sample

$V_V=18.86[in^3]$, $V_T=62.58[in^3]$ } volume of voids and total volume of the sand

$A_g=12.57[in^2]$ ↑ gross area of the permeameter

A) 120[ft/day]
B) 130[ft/day]
C) 140[ft/day]
D) 150[ft/day]

Problem #29

Find: ΔN_E ← the minimum number of engineers to be added to the team so that engineering is no longer the bottleneck task.

Given:

predecessor task of task i → $Pred_i$; the number of people working on task i, [workers] → N_i; production rate of task i, [acres/(hour*workers)] → U_i

i	$Task_i$	$Pred_i$	N_i	U_i
S	Surveying	-	8	0.10
E	Engineering	S	4	0.12
G	Grading	E	26	0.04

A) 2
B) 3
C) 4
D) 5

Problem #30

Find: Q_{30-40} ← the flow rate between minute 30 and minute 40

Given:

$V_T=3.321*10^5[gal]$ ↑ total volume of runoff from minute 0 to minute 60

$A_{shed}=57[acres]$ ↑ area of watershed

A) 16[ft³/s]
B) 17[ft³/s]
C) 18[ft³/s]
D) 19[ft³/s]

Problem #31

Find: τ @ σ=3,000[lb/ft^2] ← the shear stress of the soil in a direct shear test when 3,000 pounds per foot of normal stress is applied

Given:

σ_1=180[lb/in^2] ← major principle stress; triaxial test results

σ_3=60[lb/in^2] ← minor principle stress; triaxial test results

A) 1,500[lb/ft^2]

B) 1,730[lb/ft^2]

C) 2,620[lb/ft^2]

D) 5,200[lb/ft^2]

Problem #32

Find: v_i ← the initial velocity of the car

Given:

S=45.5[m] ← stopping sight distance

t_p=2.5[s] ← perception-reaction time

a=3.1[m/s^2] ← acceleration (the car slowing down to a stop)

G=4% (uphill) ← grade

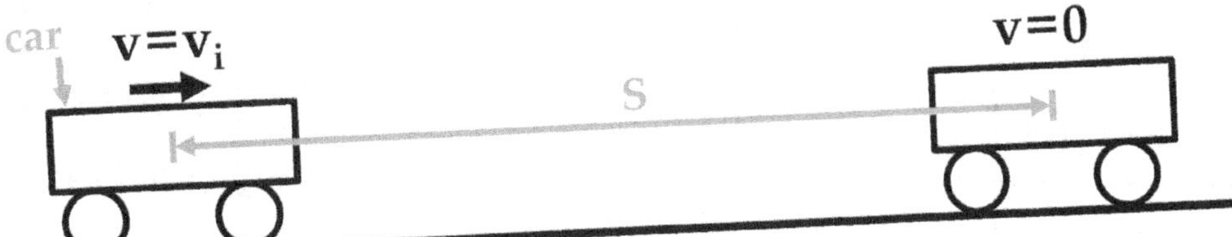

A) 40[km/hr]

B) 50[km/hr]

C) 60[km/hr]

D) 70[km/hr]

Problem #33

Find: q_a ← the allowable bearing capacity

Given:

use Terzaghi bearing capacity factors

D=1[m] ← depth of footing

B=2[m] ← base width of footing

F=2 ← safety factor

ϕ=40° ← angle of internal friction

W=9,560[N]
V=0.478[m^3] } weight and volume of a sample of the soil

groundwater not present

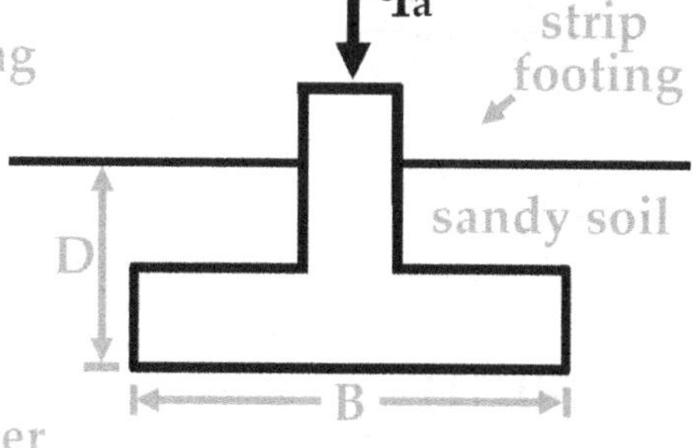

A) 1.63*10^6[N/m^2]

B) 1.82*10^6[N/m^2]

C) 2.01*10^6[N/m^2]

D) 3.63*10^6[N/m^2]

Problem #34

Find: σ_1 ← the larger principle normal stress

Given:

σ_y=-10,500[lb/in^2] ← normal stress in the y-direction (compression)

σ_x=3,400[lb/in^2] ← normal stress in the x-direction (tension)

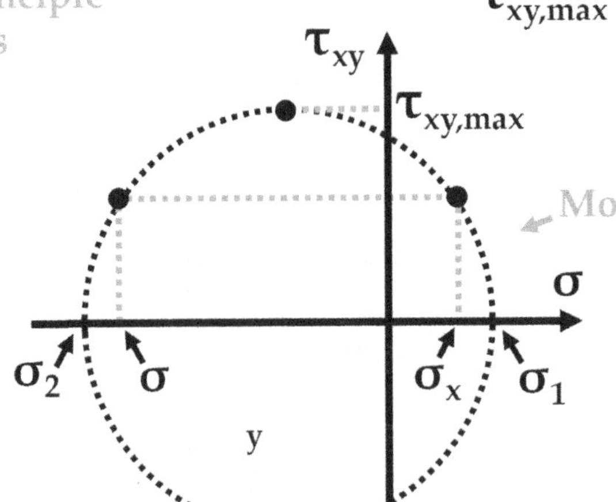

$\tau_{xy,max}$=9,050[lb/in^2] ← the maximum shear stress

A) 5,500[lb/in^2]

B) 5,800[lb/in^2]

C) 8,830[lb/in^2]

D) 9,050[lb/in^2]

Problem #35

Find: V_{nc} ← the net volume of cut material

Given: cut and fill data

STA	Cut Area	Fill Area
0+00	0[ft^2]	0[ft^2]
0+25	62[ft^2]	21[ft^2]
0+50	80[ft^2]	34[ft^2]
0+75	45[ft^2]	24[ft^2]
1+00	0[ft^2]	0[ft^2]

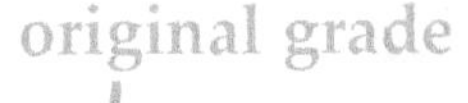

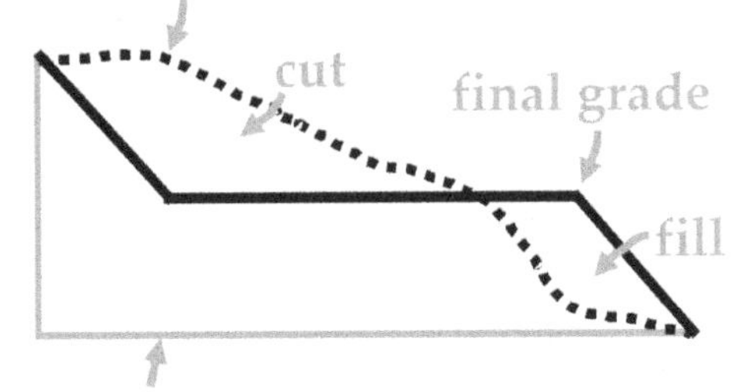

A) 100[yd^3]

B) 250[yd^3]

C) 2,000[yd^3]

D) 2,700[yd^3]

Problem #36

Find: t ← the time required to completely fill the conical tank with water.

Given:

P=2.5[hp] ← power of the pump

d_T=50[ft] ← tank diameter (at the top)

h_T=50[ft] ← tank height

η_p=80% ← pump efficiency

Δh=200[ft] ← total head lift seen by the pump

assume the tank starts empty

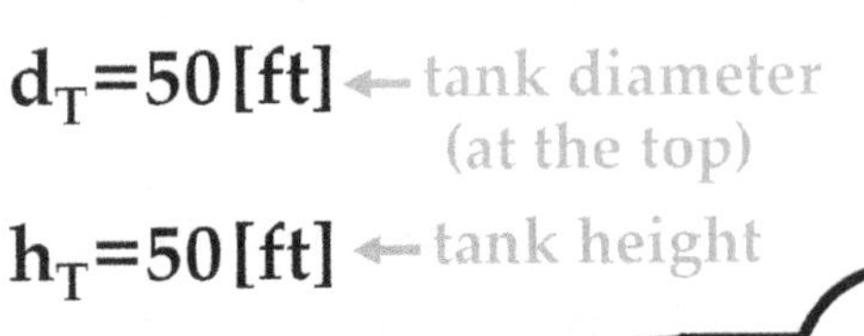

A) 1.3[days]

B) 3.4[days]

C) 4.3[days]

D) 12.9[days]

Problem #37

Find: $\tau_{max,B}$ ← the maximum shear stress in the beam at point B.

Given:

P_C=8 [k] ← the point load at point C.

L_{AD}=12 [ft]
L_{BD}=9 [ft]
L_{CD}=6 [ft]
} the length between point D and the other three points on the beam

b_w=4 [in] ← the beam width
b_h=5 [in] ← the beam height

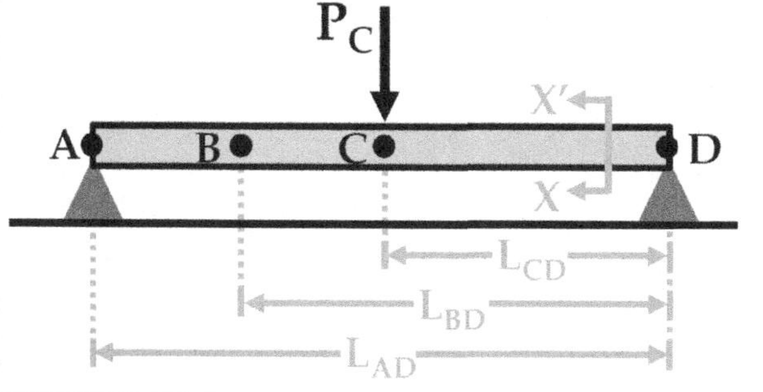

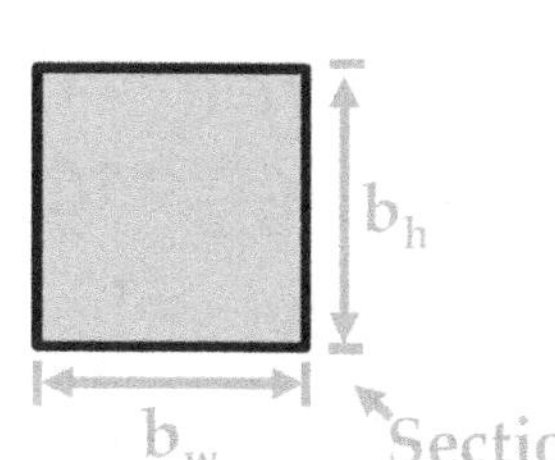

A) 0.3 [ksi]
B) 0.4 [ksi]
C) 4 [ksi]
D) 40 [ksi]

Problem #38

Find: H_B ← the height of the soil when loaded at 16,000 [lb/ft²]

Given:

H_A=1.000 [in] ← height of the sample when loaded at $\sigma_{v,A}$

ID	σ'_v [lb/ft²] (vertical effective stress)	e (void ratio)
A	8,000	1.000
B	16,000	0.914

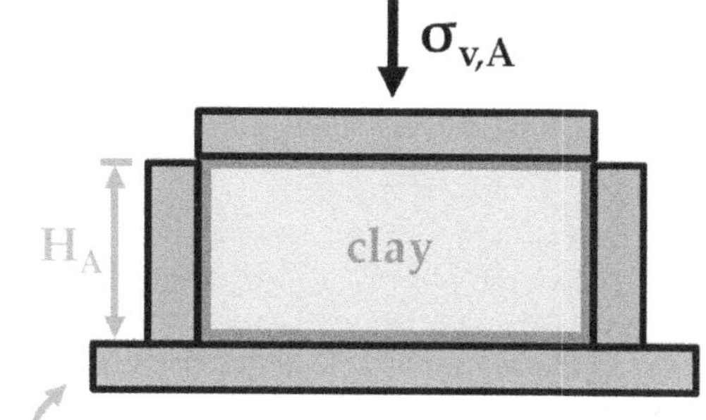

consolidation test in a consolidometer

the clay soil is normally consolidated at $\sigma_{v,A}$=8,000[lb/ft²]

A) 0.828 [in]
B) 0.914 [in]
C) 0.957 [in]
D) 1.000 [in]

Problem #39

Find: R ← the rate of grade change along the crest vertical curve

Given:

g_1=1.5% ← approach grade
g_2=-2.5% ← departing grade

a_y=-0.02*g ← vertical acceleration experienced by car passengers while driving over the curve

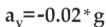

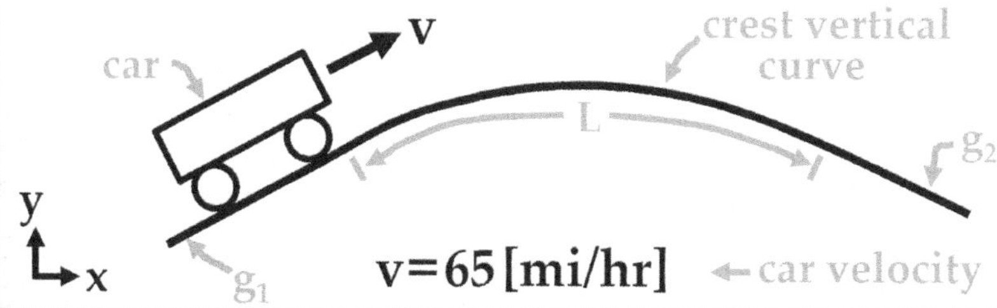

v=65 [mi/hr] ← car velocity

A) $-9.4*10^{-4}$ [%/ft]
B) $-3.8*10^{-3}$ [%/ft]
C) $-7.1*10^{-3}$ [%/ft]
D) $-2.6*10^{-2}$ [%/ft]

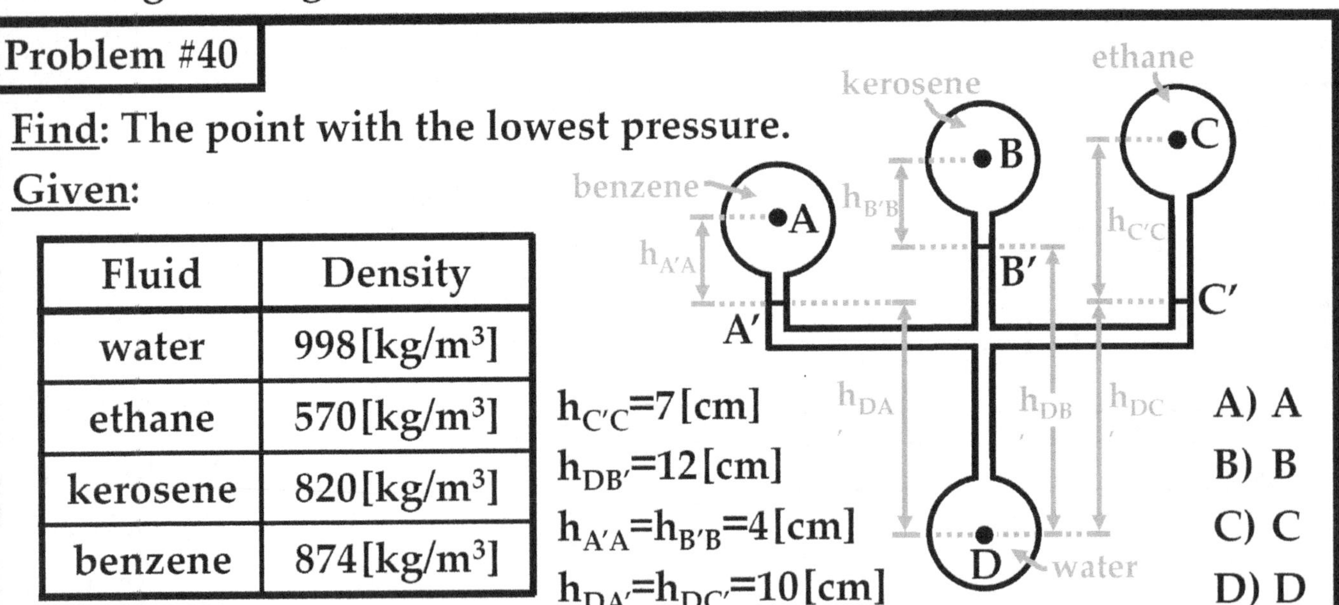

Problem #40

Find: The point with the lowest pressure.

Given:

Fluid	Density
water	998[kg/m³]
ethane	570[kg/m³]
kerosene	820[kg/m³]
benzene	874[kg/m³]

$h_{C'C}$=7[cm]

$h_{DB'}$=12[cm]

$h_{A'A}$=$h_{B'B}$=4[cm]

$h_{DA'}$=$h_{DC'}$=10[cm]

A) A

B) B

C) C

D) D

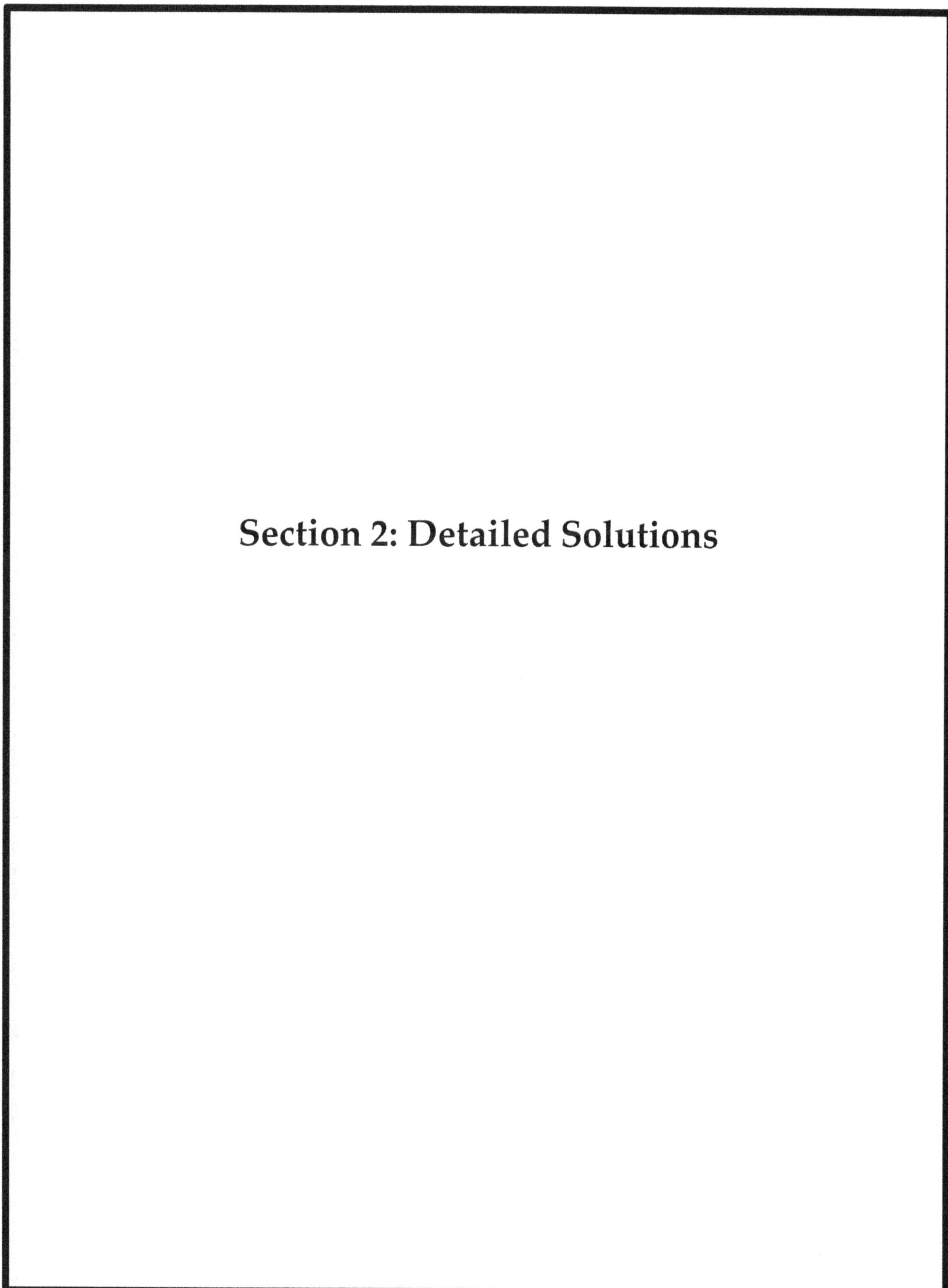

Section 2: Detailed Solutions

(page intentionally left blank)

Solution #1

Find: F_{GF} ← the force in member GF

Given:

3 [kN] 4 [kN]

B C D

cable cable

L_{DE}

G L_{GF} F L_{FE} E

$L_{DE} = 1.5\,[m]$
$L_{FE} = 2.0\,[m]$
$L_{GF} = 2.0\,[m]$
} length of members in the structure

$F_{GC} = 0\,[kN]$ ← assume 0 force in cable GC

cables only sustain a tensile force

A) 0 [kN]

B) 11.67 [kN] (tension)

C) 12.33 [kN] (compression)

D) 14.67 [kN] (compression)

Analysis:

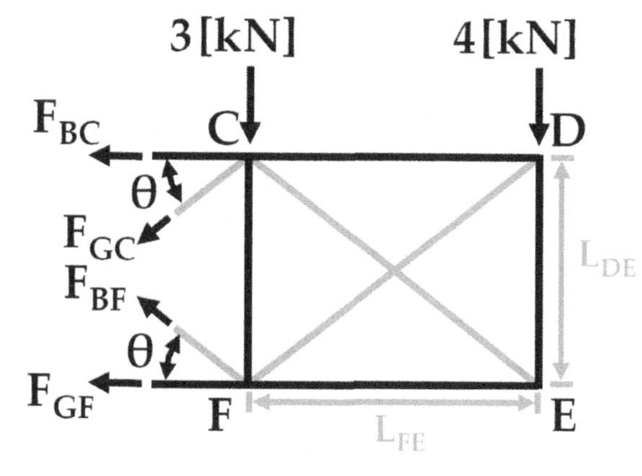

Figure 1

In Figure 1 we takes a section through members BC, GC, BF and GF.

As drawn, Figure 1 assumes all members are in tension.

Eq.1 sums the moments about point C, assuming member GF and cable BF are in tension.

$$\Sigma M_C = 0 = -4\,[kN] * L_{CD} - F_{GF} * L_{CF} - F_{BF} * L_{CF} * \cos(\theta) \quad \leftarrow eq.1$$

$$F_{GF} = \frac{-4\,[kN] * L_{CD} - F_{BF} * L_{CF} * \cos(\theta)}{L_{CF}} \quad \leftarrow eq.2$$

Solve eq.1 for F_{GF}.

$$\Sigma F_y = 0 = -3\,[kN] - 4\,[kN] + F_{BF} * \sin(\theta) - F_{GC} * \sin(\theta) \quad \leftarrow eq.3$$

To find the force in member BF, sum the forces in the vertical direction for the section shown in Figure 1.

Solution #1 (cont.)

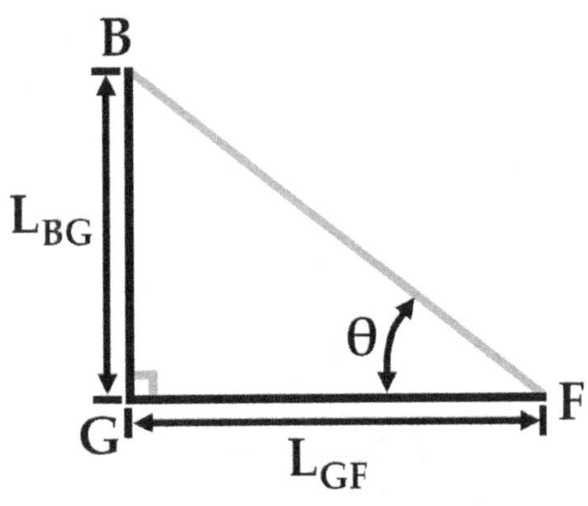

Figure 2

Use Figure 2 and trigonometry to compute angle theta, θ.

Assume triangle BFG is a right triangle, and member length BG equals member length DE.

$$L_{BG} = L_{DE} = 1.5\,[m]$$

Plug in side lengths L_{BG} and L_{GF} into eq.4, then solve for θ.

$L_{BG}=1.5\,[m]$

$$\theta = \tan^{-1}\left(\frac{L_{BG}}{L_{GF}}\right) \leftarrow eq.4$$

$L_{GF}=2.0\,[m]$

In eq.4, we're assuming $L_{BG}=L_{DE}=1.5$ meters.

$$\theta = \tan^{-1}\left(\frac{1.5\,[m]}{2.0\,[m]}\right)$$

$$\theta = 36.87^{o}$$

Solve eq.3 for F_{BF}, plug in variables F_{GC} and θ, then solve for F_{BF}.

$F_{GC}=0\,[kN]$

$$F_{BF} = \frac{3\,[kN]+4\,[kN]+F_{GC}*\sin(\theta)}{\sin(\theta)} \leftarrow eq.5$$

$\theta=36.87^{o}$

$$F_{BF} = \frac{3\,[kN]+4\,[kN]+0\,[kN]*\sin(36.87^{o})}{\sin(36.87^{o})}$$

$$F_{BF} = 11.67\,[kN]$$

(in tension)

Cable BF experiences a tensile force of 11.67 kilonewtons.

Solution #1 (cont.)

$F_{FB}=11.67\,[kN]$ $\theta=36.87^{\circ}$

$$F_{GF}=\frac{-4[kN]*L_{CD}-F_{BF}*L_{CF}*\cos(\theta)}{L_{CF}} \leftarrow eq.2$$

$L_{CD}=2\,[m]$ $L_{CF}=1.5\,[m]$

Plug in variables L_{CD}, F_{BF}, L_{CF} and θ into eq.2, then solve for F_{GF}.

$$F_{GF}=\frac{-4[kN]*2[m]-11.67[kN]*1.5[m]*\cos(36.87^{\circ})}{1.5[m]}$$

$$F_{GF}=-14.67\,[kN]$$

(in tension)

In eq.2, we assumed F_{FG} was a tensile force. Since F_{FG} computes to a negative value it is actually a compressive force.

$$F_{GF}=14.67\,[kN]$$

(in compression)

Answer: D

Solution #2

4 compaction tests were run on the same sample

Find: w_{opt} ← the optimal water content

Given: weight of water, weight of solid, total volume

laboratory test data →

Test	W_W	W_S	V_T
A	0.97 [lb]	24.11 [lb]	0.244 [ft³]
B	1.18 [lb]	19.55 [lb]	0.193 [ft³]
C	1.79 [lb]	22.45 [lb]	0.228 [ft³]
D	1.84 [lb]	18.40 [lb]	0.206 [ft³]

A) 4%
B) 6%
C) 8%
D) 10%

Analysis:

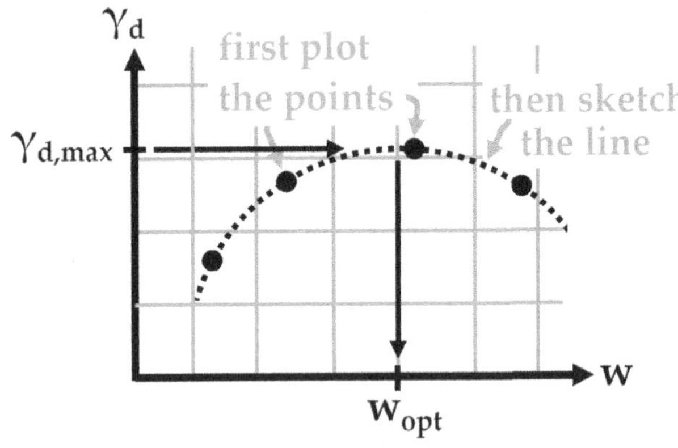

Figure 1

Using the compaction test data, we'll plot the dry unit weight vs. water content to find the optimal water content, similar to Figure 1.

The optimal water content corresponds to the maximum dry unit weight.

To plot the points, we must determine the water content and dry unit weight values.

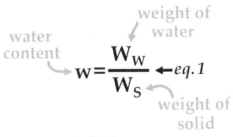

water content → $w = \dfrac{W_W}{W_S}$ ← eq. 1 (weight of water over weight of solid)

Eq. 1 is the general equation used to compute the water content.

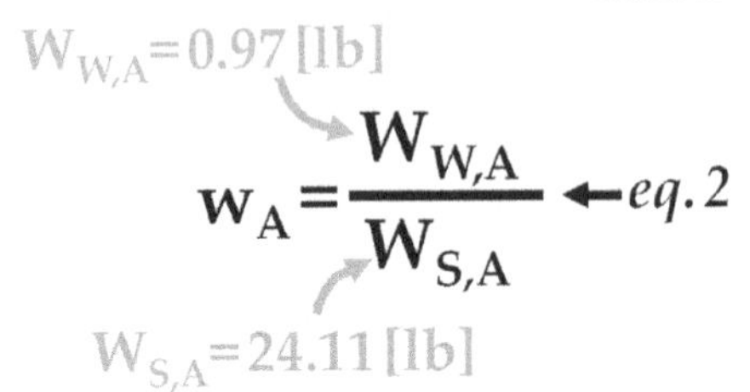

$W_{W,A}$=0.97 [lb]
$w_A = \dfrac{W_{W,A}}{W_{S,A}}$ ← eq. 2
$W_{S,A}$=24.11 [lb]

Eq. 2 computes the water content for test A.

Plug in variables $W_{W,A}$ and $W_{S,A}$ into eq. 2, then solve for w_A.

$$w_A = \frac{0.97\,[lb]}{24.11\,[lb]}$$

Solution #2 (cont.)

$$w_A = 0.040$$

$W_{W,B} = 1.18\,[lb]$

$$w_B = \frac{W_{W,B}}{W_{S,B}} \leftarrow eq.3$$

$W_{S,B} = 19.55\,[lb]$

Eq. 3 computes the water content for test B.

Plug in variables $W_{W,B}$ and $W_{S,B}$ into eq. 3, then solve for w_B.

$$w_B = \frac{1.18\,[lb]}{19.55\,[lb]}$$

$$w_B = 0.060$$

Repeat this water content calculation for tests C and D in eq. 4 and eq. 5, respectively.

$W_{W,C} = 1.79\,[lb]$

$$w_C = \frac{W_{W,C}}{W_{S,C}} \leftarrow eq.4$$

$W_{S,C} = 22.45\,[lb]$

$$w_C = \frac{1.79\,[lb]}{22.45\,[lb]}$$

$$w_C = 0.080$$

$W_{W,D} = 1.84\,[lb]$

$$w_D = \frac{W_{W,D}}{W_{S,D}} \leftarrow eq.5$$

$W_{S,D} = 18.40\,[lb]$

$$w_D = \frac{1.84\,[lb]}{18.40\,[lb]}$$

$$w_D = 0.100$$

weight of solid

$$\gamma_d = \frac{W_S}{V_T} \leftarrow eq.6$$

total volume

Eq. 6 is the general equation to compute the dry unit weight.

$W_{S,A} = 24.11\,[lb]$

$$\gamma_{d,A} = \frac{W_{S,A}}{V_{T,A}} \leftarrow eq.7$$

$V_{T,A} = 0.244\,[ft^3]$

Eq. 7 computes the dry unit weight for test A.

Plug in variables $W_{S,A}$ and $V_{T,A}$ into eq. 7, then solve for $\gamma_{d,A}$

Solution #2 (cont.)

$$\gamma_{d,A}=\frac{24.11\,[lb]}{0.244\,[ft^3]}$$

$$\gamma_{d,A}=98.8\,[lb/ft^3]$$

$W_{S,B}=19.55\,[lb]$

$$\gamma_{d,B}=\frac{W_{S,B}}{V_{T,B}} \leftarrow eq.8$$

$V_{T,B}=0.193\,[ft^3]$

Eq.8 computes the dry unit weight for test B.

Plug in variables $W_{S,B}$ and $V_{T,B}$ into eq.8, then solve for $\gamma_{d,B}$.

$$\gamma_{d,B}=\frac{19.55\,[lb]}{0.193\,[ft^3]}$$

$$\gamma_{d,B}=101.3\,[lb/ft^3]$$

Repeat this dry unit weight calculation for tests C and D in eq.9 and eq.10, respectively.

$W_{S,C}=22.45\,[lb]$

$$\gamma_{d,C}=\frac{W_{S,C}}{V_{T,C}} \leftarrow eq.9$$

$V_{T,C}=0.228\,[ft^3]$

$$\gamma_{d,C}=\frac{22.45\,[lb]}{0.228\,[ft^3]}$$

$$\gamma_{d,C}=98.5\,[lb/ft^3]$$

$W_{S,D}=18.40\,[lb]$

$$\gamma_{d,D}=\frac{W_{S,D}}{V_{T,D}} \leftarrow eq.10$$

$V_{T,D}=0.213\,[ft^3]$

$$\gamma_{d,D}=\frac{18.40\,[lb]}{0.206\,[ft^3]}$$

$$\gamma_{d,D}=89.3\,[lb/ft^3]$$

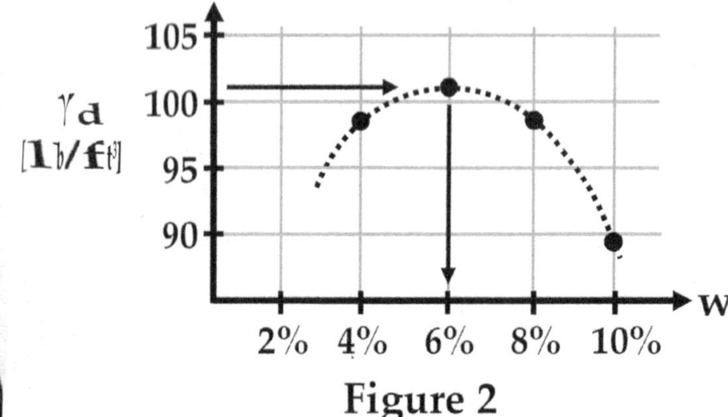

Figure 2

Plot the water content and dry unit weight values of all four tests, then sketch a best fit curve and identify the optimum water content, which is 6%.

Answer: B

Solution #3

Find: d ← the depth of flow in the channel

Given:

n=0.017 ← roughness coefficient

b=4[m] ← base width

v=3.1[m/s] ← channel velocity

S=0.001 ← channel slope

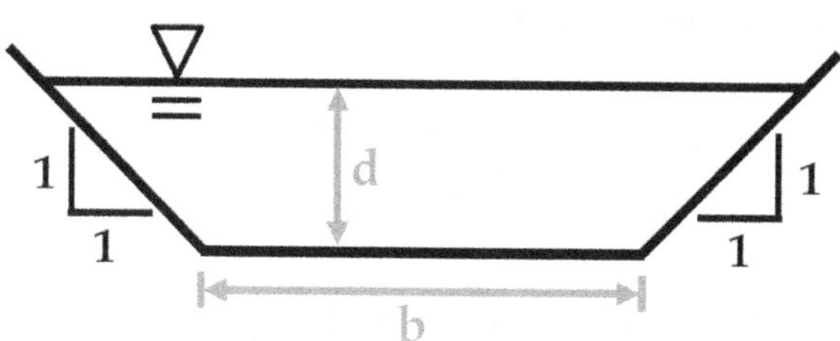

trapezoidal channel

the channel side slopes are 1:1

A) 1.2[m]

B) 1.5[m]

C) 1.8[m]

D) 4.2[m]

Analysis:

$$v = \frac{k}{n} * R^{2/3} * S^{1/2} \quad \leftarrow eq.1$$

(v: channel velocity; k: conversion factor; n: roughness coefficient; R: hydraulic radius; S: channel slope)

Eq.1 computes the channel velocity.

$$R = \left(\frac{v * n}{k * S^{1/2}}\right)^{1.5} \quad \leftarrow eq.2$$

(v=3.1[m/s], n=0.017, k=1[m^{1/3}/s], S=0.001)

Solve eq.1 for the hydraulic radius, R, then plug in variables v, n, k and S, then solve for R.

$$R = \left(\frac{3.1[m/s] * 0.017}{1[m^{1/3}/s] * (0.001)^{1/2}}\right)^{1.5}$$

(R=A/P)

The hydraulic radius equals the cross-sectional area of the channel divided by the wetted perimeter.

$$\frac{A}{P} = 2.151[m] \quad \leftarrow eq.3$$

(A: channel area; P: wetted perimeter)

The channel area and wetted perimeter are both functions of the channel depth.

$$A = b*d + 2*0.5*d*1*d \quad \leftarrow eq.4$$

(b=4[m]; b*d: rectangular area; 2*0.5*d*1*d: area of 2 triangles; 1: side slope)

Eq.4 computes the channel area as the rectangular area plus the two triangular areas.

Solution #3 (cont.)

$$A = 4[m] * d + d^2$$

$$P = b + 2 * d\sqrt{2} \leftarrow eq.5$$

$b = 4[m]$

Eq.5 computes the wetted perimeter of the channel.

$$P = 4[m] + 2 * d\sqrt{2}$$

$A = 4[m]*d + d^2$

$$\frac{A}{P} = 2.151[m] \leftarrow eq.3$$

$P = 4[m] + 2*d\sqrt{2}$

Plug in the equations for the channel area and wetted perimeter into eq.3.

$$\frac{4[m] * d + d^2}{4[m] + 2 * d\sqrt{2}} = 2.151[m] \leftarrow eq.6$$

"LHS"

Plug in the four possible values for the depth into the left hand side (LHS) of eq.6. Whichever value of d makes the LHS closest to 2.151 meters is correct.

d	LHS
1.2[m]	0.84[m]
1.5[m]	1.00[m]
1.8[m]	1.15[m]
4.2[m]	2.14[m]

Answer: D

A depth of 4.2 feet generates a LHS value most nearly 2.151 meters.

Solution #4

Find: A_1 ← the annual cash flow for years 1 through 17

Given:

$i=7.5\%$ ← nominal interest rate (quarterly compounding)

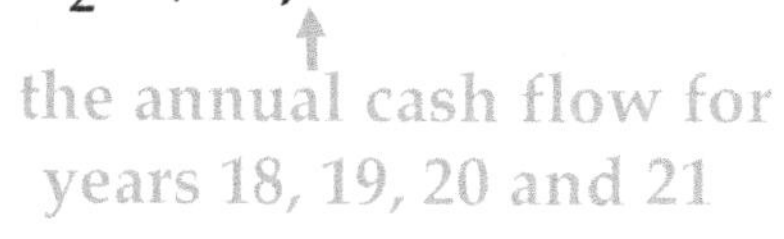

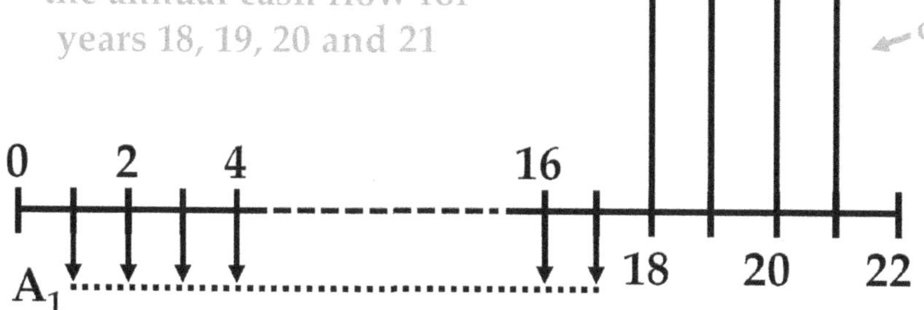

A) \$1,000

B) \$1,014

C) \$1,038

D) \$1,054

Analysis:

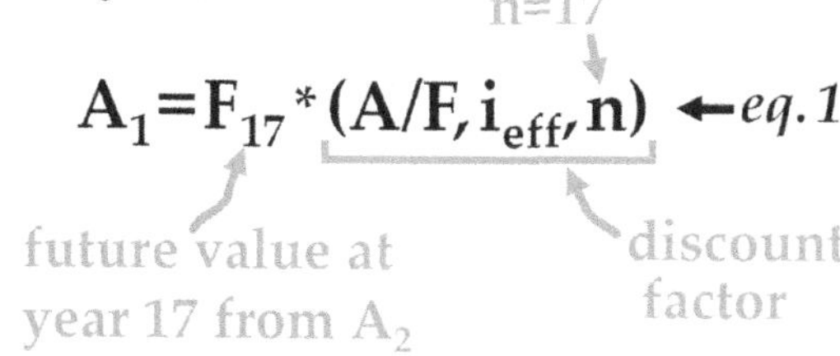

The annual cash flow for years 1 through 17 equals the equivalent future value at year 17 from cash flow A_2, times the appropriate uniform series discount factor.

$$A_1=F_{17}*(A/F,i_{eff},17)$$

For eq.1, we know the number of years equals 17 (n=17).

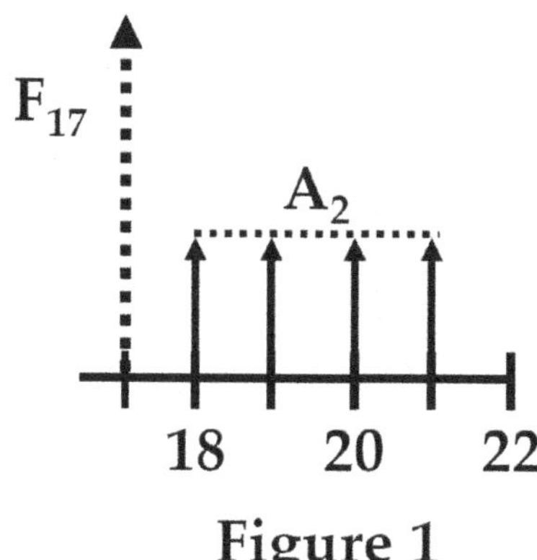

Figure 1

Figure 1 shows cash flow F_{17}, which is equivalent to the positive cash flow for years 18, 19, 20 and 21.

Cash flow problems like this one typically assume there is no cash in the account at the beginning (year 0) or at the end (year 22) of the cash flow diagram.

$$F_{17}=A_2*(P/A,i_{eff},n) \leftarrow eq.2$$

n=4; A_2: annual positive cash flow; $(P/A,i_{eff},n)$: discount factor

Eq. 2 computes the value of F_{17}, where n=4.

Solution #4 (cont.)

$$(P/A, i_{eff}, 4) = \frac{(1+i_{eff})^n - 1}{i_{eff} * (1+i_{eff})^n} \leftarrow eq.3$$

effective annual interest rate; number of years

Eq.3 computes the discount factor used in eq.2, which is a function of the effective annual interest rate and the number of years.

$$i_{eff} = (1+i/m)^m \leftarrow eq.4$$

$i = 7.5\% = 0.075$ $m = 4$

Eq.4 computes the effective annual interest rate based on the nominal interest rate and compounding period.

$$i_{eff} = (1+0.075/4)^4$$

For quarterly compounding, m=4

$$i_{eff} = 0.07713$$

Plug in i_{eff} and n into eq.3, then solve for the discount factor.

$$(P/A, i_{eff}, 4) = \frac{(1+i_{eff})^n - 1}{i_{eff} * (1+i_{eff})^n} \leftarrow eq.3$$

$i_{eff} = 0.07713$ $n = 4$

$$(P/A, 7.713\%, 4) = \frac{(1+0.07713)^4 - 1}{0.07713 * (1+0.07713)^4}$$

$$(P/A, 7.713\%, 4) = 3.333396$$

Plug in A_2 and (P/A,7.713%,4) into eq.2, then solve for F_{17}.

$$F_{17} = A_2 * (P/A, 7.713\%, 4) \leftarrow eq.2$$

$A_2 = \$10,000$ $(P/A, 7.713\%, 4) = 3.333396$

$$F_{17} = \$10,000 * 3.333396$$

$$F_{17} = \$33,334$$

Solution #4 (cont.)

Eq.5 computes the discount factor used in eq.1.

$$(A/F,7.713\%,17)=\frac{i_{eff}}{(1+i_{eff})^{n}-1} \leftarrow eq.5$$

$i_{eff}=0.07713$ $n=17$

Plug in the values of i_{eff}, and n into eq.5, then solve for (A/F,7.713%,17)

$$(A/F,7.713\%,17)=\frac{0.07713}{(1+0.07713)^{17}-1}$$

$$(A/F,7.713\%,17)=0.03041$$

Plug in the values of F_{17} and (A/F,7.713%,17) into eq.1, then solve for A_1.

$$A_1=F_{17}*(A/F,7.713\%,17) \leftarrow eq.1$$

$F_{17}=\$33,334$ $(A/F,7.713\%,17)=0.03041$

$$A_1=\$33,334*0.03041$$

$$A_1=\$1,014$$

Answer: B

Solution #5

Find: $M_{x=5[m]}$ ← the moment at the mid-span of the beam

Given:

$P_A = P_C = 8[kN]$ ← load at points A and E

$L_{AB} = 2[m]$
$L_{AC} = 3[m]$
$L_{CE} = 7[m]$
$L_{DE} = 2[m]$
} length between two specified points along the beam

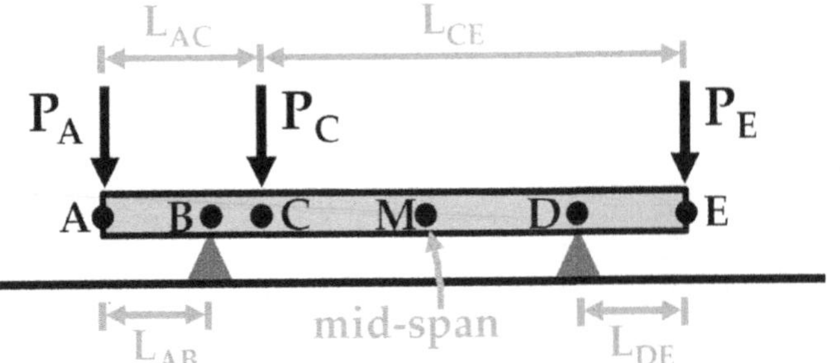

$P_E = 20[kN]$
load at point E

A) 16[kN*m]
B) -13[kN*m]
C) -16[kN*m]
D) -24[kN*m]

Analysis:

$$M_{x=5[m]} = \sum_{0}^{5} F * L \leftarrow eq.1$$

(shear force; length along the beam)

Eq.1 computes the moment at the mid-span of the beam as the sum product of the shear force times the length along the beam.

Eq.2 expands the summation from eq.1.

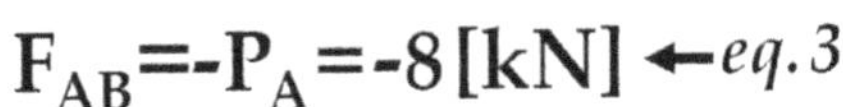

$$M_{x=5[m]} = F_{AB} * L_{AB} + F_{BC} * L_{BC} + F_{CM} * L_{CM} \leftarrow eq.2$$

(shear forces; lengths)

F_{AB} is the shear force in the beam along length L_{AB}. F_{BC} is the shear force in the beam along length L_{BC}. F_{CM} is the shear force in the beam along length L_{CM}.

$$F_{AB} = -P_A = -8[kN] \leftarrow eq.3$$

$$F_{BC} = -P_A + R_B \leftarrow eq.4$$

$$F_{CM} = -P_A + R_B - P_C \leftarrow eq.5$$

Eq.3, eq.4 and eq.5 compute the shear force values to be used in eq.2.

Figure 1 identifies the 5 forces acting vertically on the beam.

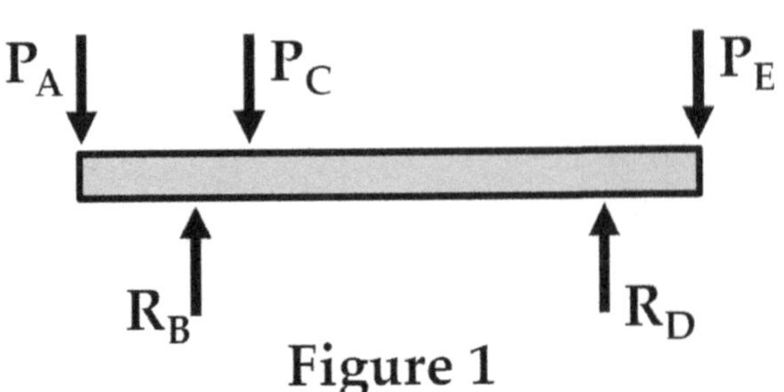

Figure 1

Solution #5 (cont.)

Eq.6 sets the moment at the pin connection at point B equal to zero, to find the reaction force at point D.

$$\Sigma M_B=0=P_A*L_{AB}-P_C*L_{BC}+R_D*L_{BD}-P_E*L_{BE} \leftarrow eq.6$$

$$R_D=\frac{-P_A*L_{AB}+P_C*L_{BC}+P_E*L_{BE}}{L_{BD}} \leftarrow eq.7$$

Solve eq.6 for the reaction force at point D.

Figure 2

Figure 2 identifies the lengths between point B and the other points along the beam.

$$L_{BC}=L_{AC}-L_{AB} \leftarrow eq.8$$

$L_{AC}=3[m]$ $L_{AB}=2[m]$

Eq.8 computes the length between points B and C.

$$L_{BC}=3[m]-2[m]$$

$$L_{BC}=1[m]$$

$$L_{BE}=L_{BC}+L_{CE} \leftarrow eq.9$$

$L_{BC}=1[m]$ $L_{CE}=7[m]$

Eq.9 computes the length between points B and E.

$$L_{BE}=1[m]+7[m]$$

$$L_{BE}=8[m]$$

$$L_{BD}=L_{BE}-L_{DE} \leftarrow eq.10$$

$L_{BE}=8[m]$ $L_{DE}=2[m]$

Eq.10 computes the length between points B and D.

$$L_{BD}=8[m]-2[m]$$

$$L_{BD}=6[m]$$

Solution #5 (cont.)

$L_{AB}=2[m]$ $L_{BC}=1[m]$ $L_{BE}=8[m]$

$P_A=8[kN]$ $P_C=8[kN]$ $P_E=20[kN]$

$$R_D=\frac{-P_A*L_{AB}+P_C*L_{BC}+P_E*L_{BE}}{L_{BD}} \leftarrow eq.7$$

$L_{BD}=6[m]$

Plug in the known values into eq.7, then solve for the reaction force at point D.

$$R_D=\frac{-(8[kN])*2[m]+8[kN]*1[m]+20[kN]*8[m]}{6[m]}$$

$$R_D=25.33[kN]$$

$$\Sigma F_y=0=-P_A+R_B-P_C+R_D-P_E \leftarrow eq.11$$

Eq. 11 sets the sum of the vertical forces equal to zero, in order to determine the reaction force R_B.

$P_C=8[kN]$ $R_D=25.33[kN]$

$$R_B=P_A+P_C+P_E-R_D$$

$P_A=8[kN]$ $P_E=20[kN]$

Solve eq.11 for R_B, then plug in variables P_A, P_C, P_E and R_D, then solve for the reaction force at point B.

$$R_B=8[kN]+8[kN]+20[kN]-25.33[kN]$$

$$R_B=10.67[kN]$$

$$F_{BC}=-P_A+R_B \leftarrow eq.4$$

$P_A=8[kN]$ $R_B=10.67[kN]$

Plug in P_A and R_B into eq.4, then solve for the shear force in the beam between points B and C, F_{BC}.

$$F_{BC}=-(8[kN])+10.67[kN]$$

$$F_{BC}=2.67[kN]$$

Solution #5 (cont.)

R_B=10.67 [kN]

$$F_{CM} = -P_A + R_B - P_C \leftarrow eq.5$$

P_A=8 [kN] P_C=8 [kN]

Plug in P_A, R_B, and P_C into eq.5, then solve for the shear force in the beam between points C and M, F_{CM}.

$$F_{CM} = -(8\,[kN]) + 10.67\,[kN] - (8\,[kN])$$

$$F_{CM} = -5.33\,[kN]$$

F_{AB}=-8 [kN] F_{BC}=2.67 [kN] F_{CM}=-5.33 [kN]

$$M_{x=5[m]} = F_{AB} * L_{AB} + F_{BC} * L_{BC} + F_{CM} * L_{CM} \leftarrow eq.2$$

L_{AB}=2 [m] L_{BC}=1 [m] L_{CM}=2 [m]

Plug in the known values into the right hand side of eq.2, then solve for the moment at the mid-span of the beam.

$$M_{x=5[m]} = -8\,[kN] * 2\,[m] + 2.67\,[kN] * 1\,[m] + (-5.33\,[kN]) * 2\,[m]$$

$$M_{x=5[m]} = -24\,[kN*m]$$

Answer: D

Solution #6

Find: STA_B ← the stationing at point B

Given: $STA_A = 4+50$ ← the stationing at point A

$L_{AC} = 58.0[ft]$ ← distance between points A and C

$I = 28.5°$ ↑ interior angle

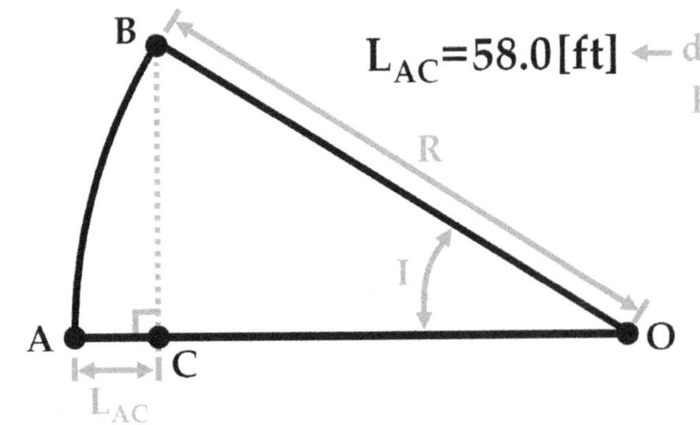

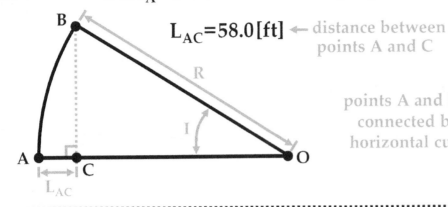

points A and B are connected by a horizontal curve.

A) 4+79

B) 5+05

C) 6+53

D) 6+88

Analysis:

$$STA_B = STA_A + L_{AB} \quad \leftarrow eq.1$$

stationing at points B and A; length along the curve from point A to point B

Eq.1 computes the stationing at point B, by adding the stationing at point A to the curve length.

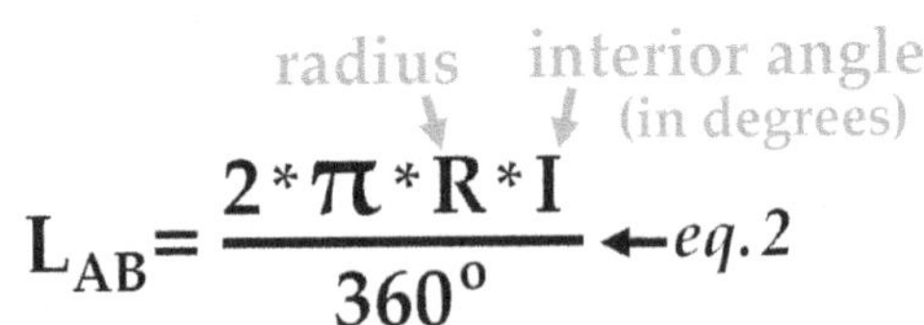

$$L_{AB} = \frac{2 * \pi * R * I}{360°} \quad \leftarrow eq.2$$

Eq.2 computes the curve length as a function of the curve radius and interior angle.

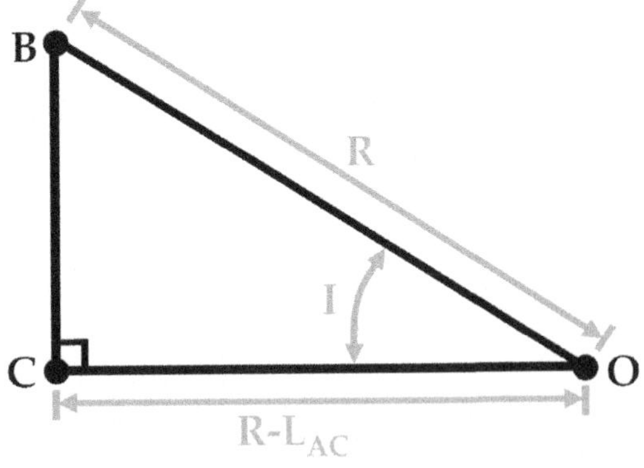

Figure 1

Figure 1 shows right triangle OCB.

$$\cos(I) = \frac{R - L_{AC}}{R} \quad \leftarrow eq.3$$

Eq.3 relates the interior angle with the curve radius and the curve length between points B and C.

Solution #6 (cont.)

$$R = \frac{L_{AC}}{1-\cos(I)} \leftarrow eq.4$$

$L_{AC}=58.0[ft]$, $I=28.5°$

Solve eq. 3 for the radius, R.

Plug in variables I and L_{AC} into eq. 4, then solve for R.

$$R = \frac{58.0[ft]}{1-\cos(28.5°)}$$

$$R=478.6[ft]$$

$R=478.6[ft]$, $I=28.5°$

$$L_{AB} = \frac{2*\pi*R*I}{360°} \leftarrow eq.2$$

Plug in variables R and I into eq. 2, then solve for L_{AB}.

$$L_{AB} = \frac{2*\pi*478.6[ft]*28.5°}{360°}$$

$$L_{AB}=238[ft]$$

$STA_A=450[ft]$, $L_{AB}=238[ft]$

$$STA_B=STA_A+L_{AB} \leftarrow eq.1$$

Plug in variables STA_A and L_{AB} into eq. 1, then solve for STA_B.

$$STA_B=450[ft]+238[ft]$$

Convert STA_A from 4+50 to 450[ft].

$$STA_B=688[ft]$$

Convert STA_B from 688[ft] to 6+88.

$$STA_B=6+88$$

Answer: D

Solution #7

Find: w_{clay} ← the water content of the clay layer

Given:

$d_{sand}=10[m]$ ← thickness of the sand layer

$d_{clay}=10[m]$ ← thickness of the clay layer

$\gamma_{T,clay}=18.15[kN/m^3]$ ← total unit weight of the clay layer

$SG_{clay}=2.65$ ← specific gravity of the clay layer

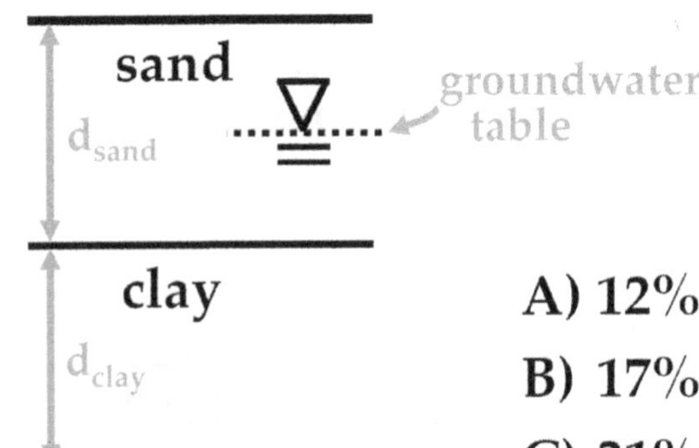

A) 12%
B) 17%
C) 21%
D) 35%

Analysis:

$W_{W,clay}=V_{W,clay}*\gamma_W$ — weight of water in the clay layer

$$w_{clay}=\frac{W_{W,clay}}{W_{S,clay}} \quad \leftarrow eq.1$$

$W_{S,clay}=V_{S,clay}*\gamma_S$ — weight of solid in the clay layer

Eq.1 computes the water content of the clay layer.

Substitute in the volume times the unit weight into eq.1, for the weight of water and solid material.

$$w_{clay}=\frac{V_{W,clay}*\gamma_W}{V_{S,clay}*\gamma_S} \quad \leftarrow eq.2$$

(water; solid)

Subscripts "W", "S", "A" and "T" refer to water, solid, air, and total, respectively.

volume of water, solid and air in the clay layer

$$V_{T,clay}=V_{W,clay}+V_{S,clay}+V_{A,clay} \quad \leftarrow eq.3$$

total volume of the clay layer

Eq.3 computes the total volume of the clay layer, which is the sum of the volumes of water, solid and air.

$$\text{assume} \rightarrow V_{T,clay}=1.00[m^3]$$

For this problem, we'll assume a representative sample of clay has a total volume of 1 cubic meter.

$$V_{A,clay}=0[m^3]$$

Since the groundwater table is above the clay layer, the volume of air is zero.

Solution #7 (cont.)

$V_{T,clay}=1.00\,[m^3]$ $V_{A,clay}=0\,[m^3]$

$$V_{T,clay}=V_{W,clay}+V_{S,clay}+V_{A,clay} \leftarrow eq.3$$

Plug in $V_{T,clay}$ and $V_{A,clay}$ into eq. 3, then solve for $V_{S,clay}$.

$$1.00\,[m^3]=V_{W,clay}+V_{S,clay}+0\,[m^3]$$

$$V_{S,clay}=1.00\,[m^3]-V_{W,clay} \leftarrow eq.4$$

Eq. 5 computes the total unit weight of the clay layer as a combination of the unit weights of the water, solid and air.

$$\gamma_{T,clay}=\gamma_{W,clay}*\left(\frac{V_{W,clay}}{V_{T,clay}}\right)+\gamma_{S,clay}*\left(\frac{V_{S,clay}}{V_{T,clay}}\right)+\gamma_{A,clay}*\left(\frac{V_{A,clay}}{V_{T,clay}}\right) \leftarrow eq.5$$

$$\gamma_{S,clay}=SG_{clay}*\gamma_W \leftarrow eq.6$$

$SG_{clay}=2.65$ $\gamma_W=9.81\,[kN/m^3]$

Eq. 6 computes the unit weight of the solid material in the clay layer.

Assume the unit weight of water equals 9.81 kilonewtons per meter cubed.

$$\gamma_{S,clay}=2.65*9.81\,[kN/m^3]$$

$$\gamma_{S,clay}=26.00\,[kN/m^3]$$

Plug in variables $\gamma_{T,clay}$, $\gamma_{W,clay}$, $\gamma_{S,clay}$, $V_{S,clay}$, $V_{A,clay}$, and $V_{T,clay}$ into eq. 5, then solve for $V_{W,clay}$.

$\gamma_{S,clay}=26.00\,[kN/m^3]$ $\gamma_{W,clay}=9.81\,[kN/m^3]$ $V_{S,clay}=1.00\,[m^3]-V_{W,clay}$ $V_{A,clay}=0\,[m^3]$

$$\gamma_{T,clay}=\gamma_{W,clay}*\left(\frac{V_{W,clay}}{V_{T,clay}}\right)+\gamma_{S,clay}*\left(\frac{V_{S,clay}}{V_{T,clay}}\right)+\gamma_{A,clay}*\left(\frac{V_{A,clay}}{V_{T,clay}}\right) \leftarrow eq.5$$

$\gamma_{T,clay}=18.15\,[kN/m^3]$ $V_{T,clay}=1.00\,[m^3]$

Since $V_{A,clay}$ equals 0, the final term in eq. 5 cancels out.

$$18.15\,[kN/m^3]=9.81\,[kN/m^3]*\left(\frac{V_{W,clay}}{1.00\,[m^3]}\right)$$

$$+\,26.00\,[kN/m^3]*\left(\frac{1.00\,[m^3]-V_{W,clay}}{1.00\,[m^3]}\right)$$

Solution #7 (cont.)

$$V_{W,clay}=0.485\,[m^3]$$

$$V_{S,clay}=1.00\,[m^3]-V_{W,clay} \leftarrow eq.4 \quad (V_{W,clay}=0.485\,[m^3])$$

Plug in variable $V_{W,clay}$ into eq. 4, then solve for $V_{S,clay}$.

$$V_{S,clay}=1.00\,[m^3]-0.485\,[m^3]$$

$$V_{S,clay}=0.515\,[m^3]$$

$V_{W,clay}=0.485\,[m^3]$ $\gamma_W=9.81\,[kN/m^3]$

$$w_{clay}=\frac{V_{W,clay}*\gamma_W}{V_{S,clay}*\gamma_S} \leftarrow eq.2$$

$V_{S,clay}=0.515\,[m^3]$ $\gamma_S=26.00\,[kN/m^3]$

Plug in variables $\gamma_{W,clay}$, $\gamma_{S,clay}$, $V_{W,clay}$ and $V_{S,clay}$ into eq. 2, then solve for w_{clay}.

$$w_{clay}=\frac{0.485\,[m^3]*9.81\,[kN/m^3]}{0.515\,[m^3]*26.00\,[kN/m^3]}$$

$$w_{clay}=0.355*100\%$$

Convert the water content from a decimal to a percent.

$$w_{clay}=35.5\%$$

<u>Answer:</u> D

Solution #8

Find: LS_D ← the late start for activity D (permitting)

Given:

ID	Activity	Duration	Pred
A	Win Bid	0	-
B	Materials	3	A
C	Construction	7	B
D	Permitting	6	A
E	Inspection	2	C,D

$ES_A=1$

↑ early start for activity A (win bid)

A) 3

B) 5

C) 7

D) 11

Analysis:

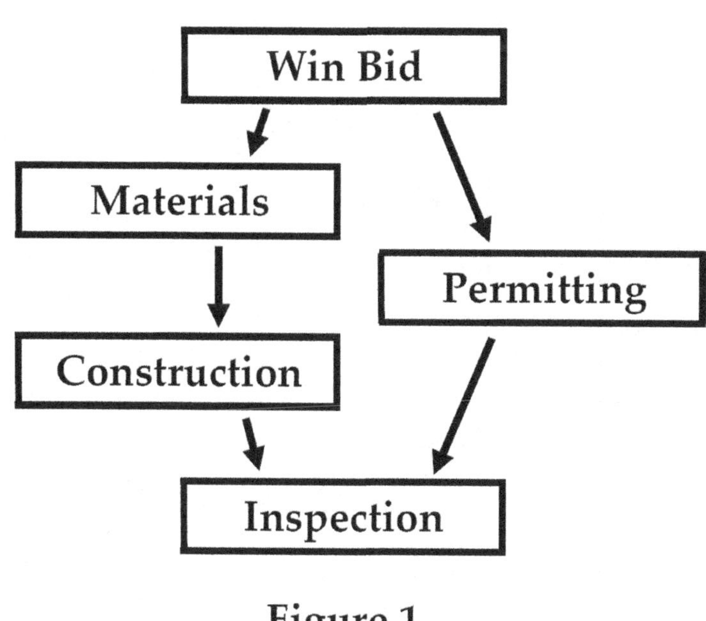

Figure 1

Figure 1 identifies the predecessor/successor relationship between the different activities within the schedule.

Win Bid		
ES_A	D_A	EF_A
LS_A	F_A	LF_A

Figure 2

Figure 2 shows the box diagram template, for Activity A. Where each box represents a time, or time period:

ES = early start
D = duration
EF = early finish
LS = late start
F = float
LF = late finish

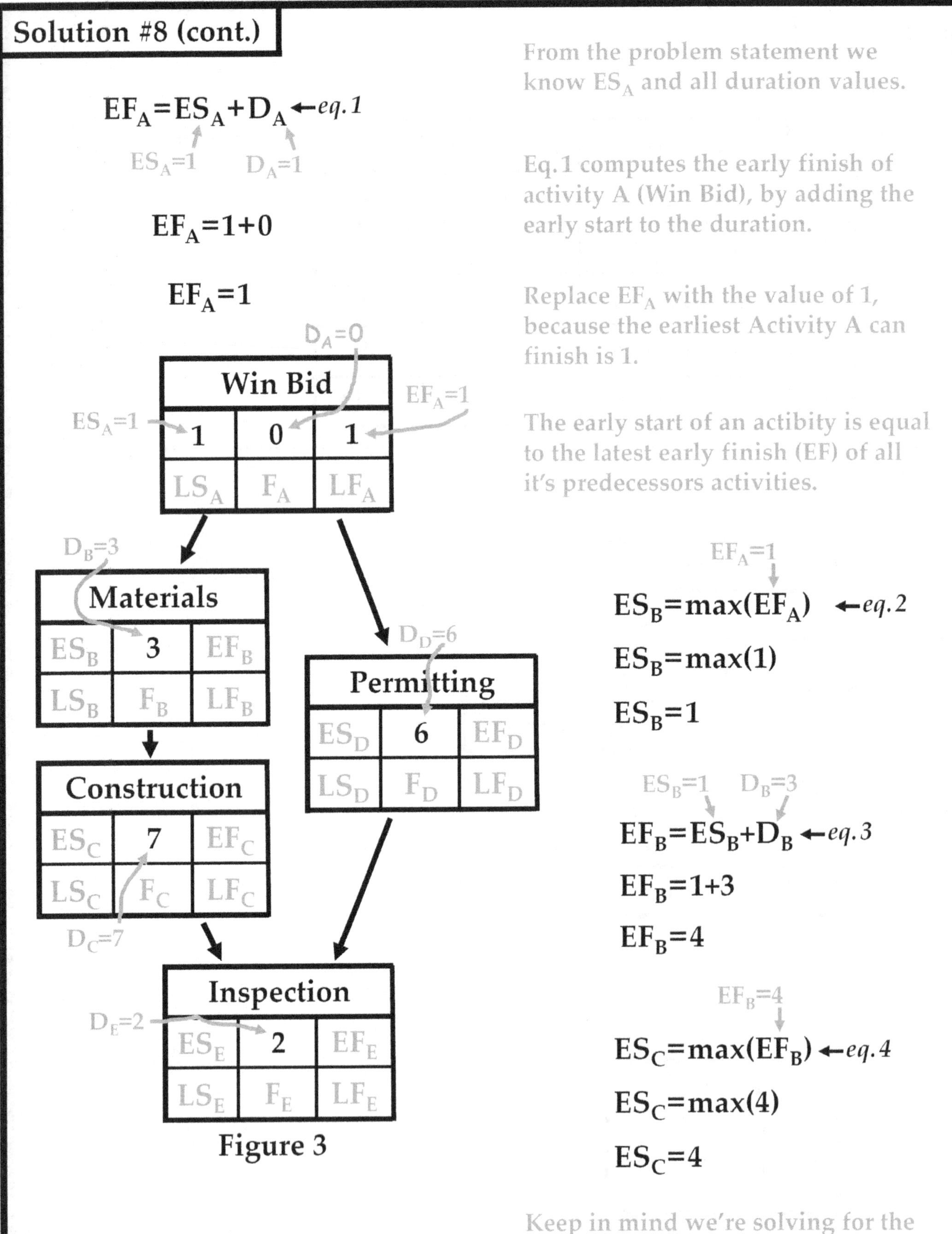

Solution #8 (cont.)

$EF_A = ES_A + D_A$ ← *eq.1* ($ES_A=1$, $D_A=1$)

From the problem statement we know ES_A and all duration values.

$EF_A = 1+0$

Eq.1 computes the early finish of activity A (Win Bid), by adding the early start to the duration.

$EF_A = 1$

Replace EF_A with the value of 1, because the earliest Activity A can finish is 1.

The early start of an actibity is equal to the latest early finish (EF) of all it's predecessors activities.

Figure 3

$ES_B = \max(EF_A)$ ← *eq.2* ($EF_A=1$)

$ES_B = \max(1)$

$ES_B = 1$

$EF_B = ES_B + D_B$ ← *eq.3* ($ES_B=1$, $D_B=3$)

$EF_B = 1+3$

$EF_B = 4$

$ES_C = \max(EF_B)$ ← *eq.4* ($EF_B=4$)

$ES_C = \max(4)$

$ES_C = 4$

Keep in mind we're solving for the late start of activity D, which we'll determine in the backward pass.

Solution #8 (cont.)

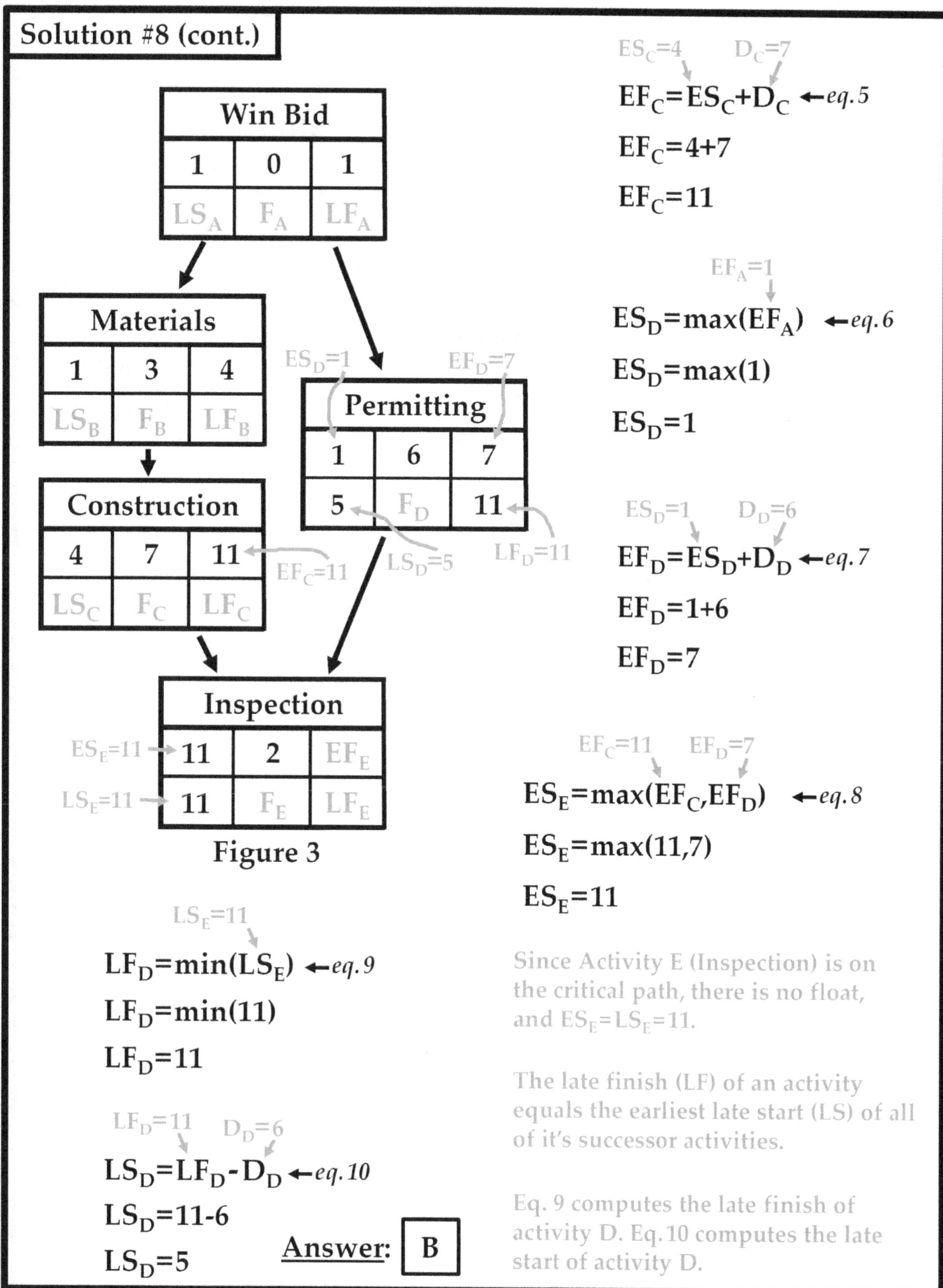

Figure 3

$ES_C=4 \quad D_C=7$

$EF_C=ES_C+D_C$ ← *eq.5*

$EF_C=4+7$

$EF_C=11$

$EF_A=1$

$ES_D=\max(EF_A)$ ← *eq.6*

$ES_D=\max(1)$

$ES_D=1$

$ES_D=1 \quad D_D=6$

$EF_D=ES_D+D_D$ ← *eq.7*

$EF_D=1+6$

$EF_D=7$

$EF_C=11 \quad EF_D=7$

$ES_E=\max(EF_C,EF_D)$ ← *eq.8*

$ES_E=\max(11,7)$

$ES_E=11$

Since Activity E (Inspection) is on the critical path, there is no float, and $ES_E=LS_E=11$.

The late finish (LF) of an activity equals the earliest late start (LS) of all of it's successor activities.

Eq. 9 computes the late finish of activity D. Eq.10 computes the late start of activity D.

$LS_E=11$

$LF_D=\min(LS_E)$ ← *eq.9*

$LF_D=\min(11)$

$LF_D=11$

$LF_D=11 \quad D_D=6$

$LS_D=LF_D-D_D$ ← *eq.10*

$LS_D=11-6$

$LS_D=5$

Answer: B

Solution #9

Find: $h_{f,AB}$ ← the headloss in the pipe between points A and B

Given:

$L_{AB}=150[ft]$ ← length of pipe AB

$Q=0.54[ft^3/s]$ ← flow rate

$v=2.75[ft/s]$ ← velocity

water flows through a smooth circular pipe

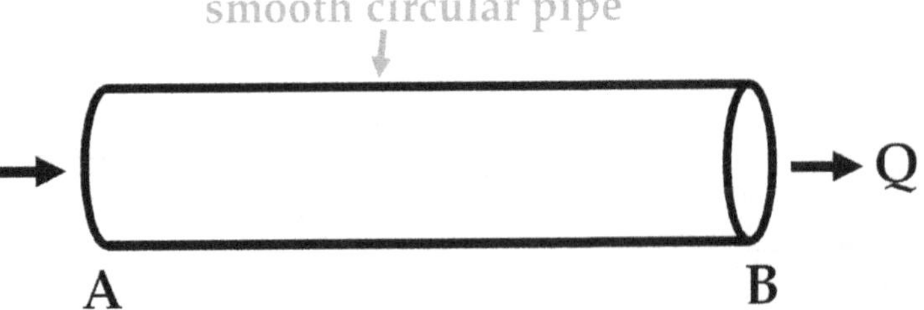

$T=68°F$ ← temperature of water

A) 0.06[ft]

B) 0.60[ft]

C) 6.00[ft]

D) 60.0[ft]

Analysis:

$$h_{f,AB}=\frac{f*L_{AB}*v^2}{2*D_e*g} \quad \leftarrow eq.1$$

headloss; friction factor; pipe length; velocity of fluid; equivalent diameter; gravitational acceleration constant

Eq.1 is the Darcy equation used to compute the headloss in the pipe from point A to point B.

For a circular cross section, the equivalent diameter equals, the diameter.

$$A=\frac{\pi*d^2}{4} \quad \leftarrow eq.2$$

cross-sectional area of pipe; diameter of pipe

Eq.2 computes the area of the pipe based on the pipe diameter.

$$d=\sqrt{\frac{4*A}{\pi}} \quad \leftarrow eq.3$$

Solve eq.2 for the pipe diameter.

$$A=Q/v \quad \leftarrow eq.4$$

$Q=0.54[ft^3/s]$ $v=2.75[ft/s]$

Eq.4 computes the cross-sectional area of the pipe as the flow rate divided by the velocity.

$$A=\frac{0.54[ft^3/s]}{2.75[ft/s]}$$

Plug in variables Q and v into eq.4, then solve for A.

$$A=0.1964[ft^2]$$

Solution #9 (cont.)

A=0.1964 [ft²]

$$d=\sqrt{\frac{4*A}{\pi}} \leftarrow eq.3$$

Plug in the pipe area into eq.3, then solve for the diameter.

$$d=\sqrt{\frac{4*0.1964[ft^2]}{\pi}}$$

$$d=0.50[ft]$$

friction factor

$$f=f(Re, \epsilon/D_e) \leftarrow eq.5$$

Reynold's number; relative roughness

Eq.5 shows the friction factor, f, is a function of Reynold's number and the relative roughness.

Figure 1

Figure 1 shows the Moody Diagram, which relates the friction factor, Reynold's number and the relative roughness.

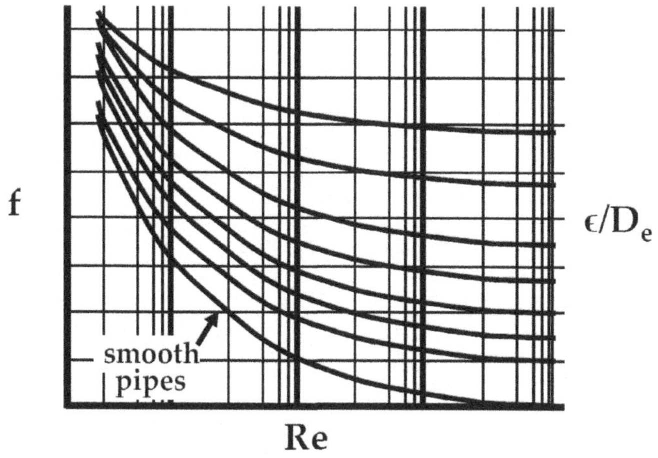

For smooth pipes, the relative roughness is assumed to be approximately 0.

fluid velocity; equivalent diameter

$$Re=\frac{v*D_e}{\nu} \leftarrow eq.6$$

Reynold's number; kinematic viscosity

Eq.6 computes Reynold's number.

$$T=68^{o}F \rightarrow \nu=1.0906*10^{-5}[ft^2/s]$$

The kinematic viscosity of a fluid depends on its temperature, and can be looked up in a table.

Solution #9 (cont.)

$v=2.75$ [ft/s] $D_e=d=0.50$ [ft]

$$Re=\frac{v*D_e}{\nu} \leftarrow eq.6$$

$\nu=1.0906*10^{-5}$ [ft²/s]

Plug in variables v, D_e and ν into eq.6, then solve for R_e.

$$Re=\frac{2.75[ft/s]*0.50[ft]}{1.0906*10^{-5}[ft^2/s]}$$

$$Re=1.26*10^5$$

Use the Moody diagram (or table refernces) to determine the friction factor of a smooth pipe, based on the Reynold's number.

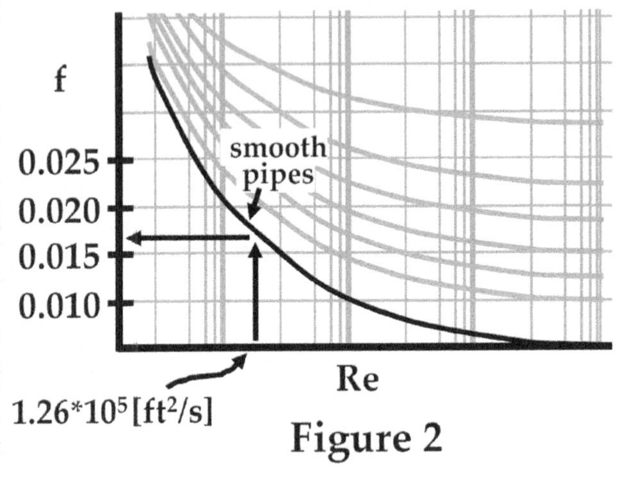

Figure 2

$$f=0.017$$

$L_{AB}=150$ [ft] $v=2.75$[ft/s] $f=0.017$

$$h_{f,AB}=\frac{f*L_{AB}*v^2}{2*D_e*g} \leftarrow eq.1$$

$D_e=d=0.50$ [ft] $g=32.2$[ft/s²]

Plug in variables f, L_{AB}, v, D_e and g into eq.1, then solve for $h_{f,AB}$.

$$h_{f,AB}=\frac{0.017*150[ft]*(2.75[ft/s])^2}{2*0.50[ft]*32.2[ft/s^2]}$$

$$h_{f,AB}=0.599[ft]$$

Answer: B

Solution #10

Find: r_2 ← the radius from the center of the well to point 2

Given:

$r_1=20[ft]$ ← distance from center of well to points 1 and 3

$r_3=100[ft]$

$s_1=4[ft]$ ← drawdown at radii 1, 2 and 3

$s_2=2[ft]$

$s_3=1[ft]$

$Y=150[ft]$ ← aquifer depth

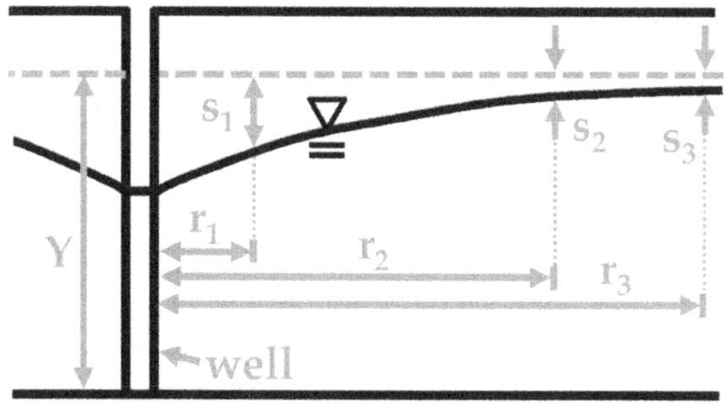

← water table for no pumping

← water table during pumping

$Q=30[gal/min]$ ← steady-state pumping rate

← unconfined aquifer

A) 58[ft]

B) 66[ft]

C) 74[ft]

D) 82[ft]

Analysis:

$$Q=\frac{\pi*K*(y_1^2-y_2^2)}{\ln(r_1/r_2)} \quad \leftarrow eq.1$$

(Q: pumping rate; K: hydraulic conductivity; y_1, y_2: aquifer depth at points 1 and 2; r_1, r_2: radius to points 1 and 2)

Eq.1 computes the steady-state flow rate from the well, based on points 1 and 2.

Solve eq.1 for r_2.

$$r_2=r_1*\left[\exp\left\{\frac{\pi*K*(y_1^2-y_2^2)}{Q}\right\}\right]^{-1} \quad \leftarrow eq.2$$

$Y=150[ft]$, $s_1=4[ft]$

$$y_1=Y-s_1 \quad \leftarrow eq.3$$

$$y_1=150[ft]-4[ft]$$

$$y_1=146[ft]$$

Eq.3 computes the aquifer depth at point 1 during pumping by subtracting the total aquifer depth, Y, from the drawdown at point 1, s_1.

$Y=150[ft]$, $s_2=2[ft]$

$$y_2=Y-s_2 \quad \leftarrow eq.4$$

$$y_2=150[ft]-2[ft]$$

$$y_2=148[ft]$$

Eq.4 computes the aquifer depth at point 2 during pumping, similar to eq.3.

Solution #10 (cont.)

aquifer depth at point 3

$$Q=\frac{\pi * K * (y_1^2-y_3^2)}{\ln(r_1/r_3)} \leftarrow eq.5$$

pumping rate

radius to point 3

Eq.5 computes the steady-state pumping rate from the well, based on points 1 and 3.

$$K=\frac{Q * \ln(r_1/r_3)}{\pi * (y_1^2-y_3^2)} \leftarrow eq.6$$

Solve eq.5 for the hydraulic conductivity, K.

Y=150[ft] s_3=1[ft]

$$y_3=Y-s_3 \leftarrow eq.7$$

Eq.7 computes the aquifer depth at point 3.

$$y_3=150[ft]-1[ft]$$

$$y_3=149[ft]$$

$$Q=30\left[\frac{gal}{min}\right] * \frac{1}{7.48}\left[\frac{ft^3}{gal}\right] \leftarrow eq.8$$

Eq.8 converts the pumping rate to units of cubic feet per minute.

$$Q=4.01[ft^3/min]$$

r_1=20[ft]

Q=4.01[ft³/min] r_3=100[ft]

$$K=\frac{Q * \ln(r_1/r_3)}{\pi * (y_1^2-y_3^2)} \leftarrow eq.6$$

y_1=146[ft] y_3=149[ft]

Plug in variables Q, r_1, r_3, y_1 and y_3 into eq.6, then solve for K.

$$K=\frac{4.01[ft^3/min] * \ln(20[ft]/100[ft])}{\pi * ((146[ft])^2-(149[ft])^2)}$$

$$K=2.321*10^{-3}[ft/min]$$

Solution #10 (cont.)

$r_1=20\,[ft]$ $y_1=146\,[ft]$ $y_2=148\,[ft]$

$$r_2=r_1*\left[\exp\left\{\frac{\pi*K*(y_1^2-y_2^2)}{Q}\right\}\right]^{-1} \leftarrow eq.2$$

$K=2.321*10^{-3}\,[ft/min]$ $Q=4.01\,[ft^3/min]$

Plug in variables r_1, K, y_1, y_2 and Q into eq.2, then solve for r_2.

$$r_2=20\,[ft]*\left[\exp\left\{\frac{\pi*2.321*10^{-3}[ft/min]*((146\,[ft])^2-(148\,[ft])^2)}{4.01\,[ft^3/min]}\right\}\right]^{-1}$$

$r_2=58.3\,[ft]$

Answer: A

Solution #11

Find: $Elev_D$ ← the elevation at point D

Given:

i	STA_i	$Elev_i$
A	10+00	243.0[ft]
B	12+00	239.0[ft]
C	STA_C	237.0[ft]
D	15+00	$Elev_D$
E	16+00	$Elev_E$

A) 237.5[ft]

B) 238.0[ft]

C) 238.5[ft]

D) 239.0[ft]

Analysis:

$$Elev_D = Elev_B + g_1 * L_{BD} + 0.5 * R * L_{BD}^2 \quad \leftarrow eq.1$$

elevation of point D; elevation of point B; approach grade; length between points B and D; rate of grade change

Eq.1 computes the elevation at point D.

$Elev_B=239.0[ft]$ $Elev_A=243.0[ft]$

$$g_1 = \frac{Elev_B - Elev_A}{STA_B - STA_A} \quad \leftarrow eq.2$$

$STA_B=1,200[ft]$ $STA_A=1,000[ft]$

Eq.2 computes the approach grade using the data from points A and B.

For eq.2, convert the stationing from 12+00 and 10+00 to 1,200 feet and 1,000 feet.

$$g_1 = \frac{239.0[ft] - 243.0[ft]}{1,200[ft] - 1,000[ft]}$$

$$g_1 = -0.02$$

$$L_{BD} = STA_D - STA_B \quad \leftarrow eq.3$$

$STA_D=1,500[ft]$ $STA_B=1,200[ft]$

Eq.3 computes the length between points B and D.

$$L_{BD} = 1,500[ft] - 1,200[ft]$$

Stationing values are converted to lengths.

Solution #11 (cont.)

$$L_{BD}=300[ft]$$

$g_C=0.00$ $g_B=-0.02$

$$R=\frac{g_C-g_B}{L_{BC}} \leftarrow eq.4$$

Eq.4 relates the rate of grade change to the curve length and approach and departing grades.

$$R=\frac{0.00-(-0.02)}{L_{BC}}$$

Plug in g_C and g_B into eq.4, then solve for R as a function of L_{BC}.

$$R=0.02/L_{BC} \leftarrow eq.5$$

Since point C is at the minimum elevation of the curve, $g_C=0$

$Elev_B=239.0[ft]$ $R=0.02/L_{BC}$

$$Elev_C=Elev_B+g_1*L_{BC}+0.5*R*L_{BC}^2 \leftarrow eq.6$$

$Elev_C=237.0[ft]$ $g_1=-0.02$

Eq.6 computes the elevation of point C. Plug in the known values and solve for L_{BC}.

$$237.0[ft]=239.0[ft]+(-0.02)*L_{BC}+0.5*(0.02/L_{BC})*L_{BC}^2$$

$$L_{BC}=200[ft]$$

$L_{BC}=200[ft]$

$$R=0.02/L_{BC} \leftarrow eq.5$$

Plug in L_{BC} into eq.5, then solve for R.

$$R=0.02/200[ft]$$

$$R=1*10^{-4}[ft^{-1}]$$

The rate of grade change equals 0.0001 per foot of length along the curve. This value is equal to 1.00% per station.

$Elev_B=239.0[ft]$ $R=1*10^{-4}[ft^{-1}]$

$$Elev_D=Elev_B+g_1*L_{BD}+0.5*R*L_{BD}^2 \leftarrow eq.1$$

$g_1=-0.02$ $L_{BD}=300[ft]$

Plug in variables $Elev_B$, g_1, L_{BD} and R into eq.1, then solve for $Elev_D$.

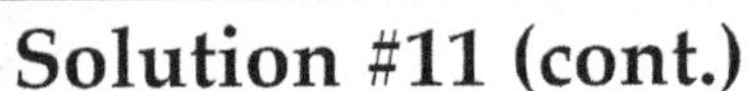

$$Elev_D = 239.0[ft] + (-0.02) * 300[ft] + 0.5 * (1 * 10^{-4}[ft^{-1}]) * (300[ft])^2$$

$$Elev_D = 237.5[ft]$$

<u>Answer</u>: **A**

Solution #12

Find: V ← the volume of material

All side slopes are 2:1 (horizontal:vertical)

Given:

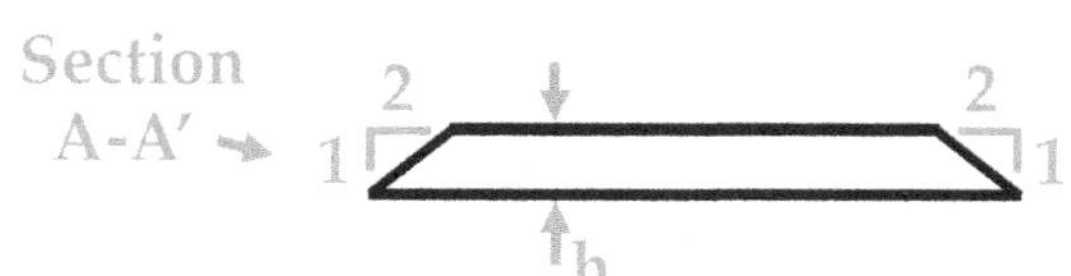

l_B=120[ft] ← base length

w_B=50[ft] ← base width

h=10[ft] ← height

A) 1,160 [yd³]

B) 1,260 [yd³]

C) 31,000 [yd³]

D) 34,000 [yd³]

Analysis:

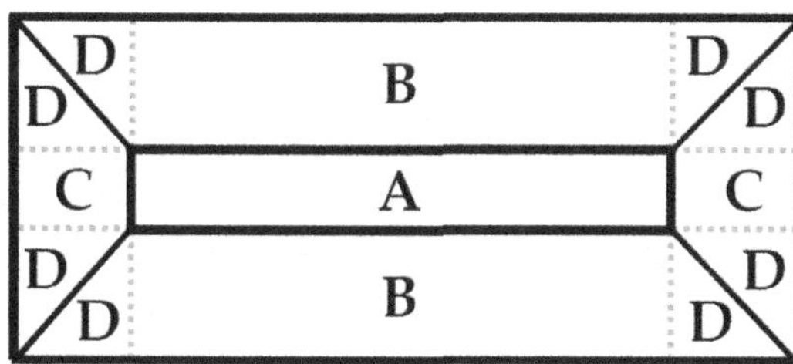

Figure 1

Figure 1 shows the volume in plan view and divides the volume into 4 unique shapes (A, B, C and D) each having a different volume.

$$V=V_A+2*V_B+2*V_C+8*V_D \leftarrow eq.1$$

Eq.1 computes the total volume based on the 4 unique shapes defined in Figure 1.

$$V_A=l_T*w_T*h \leftarrow eq.2$$

(height; l_T: length along top of volume; w_T: width along top of volume)

Eq.2 computes volume A.

$$l_T=l_B-2*2*h \leftarrow eq.3$$

(2: accounts for 2:1 side slope; 2: accounts for 2 sides; l_B=120[ft]; h=10[ft])

Eq.3 computes the length along the top of the volume.

Plug in the base length and height of the volume, then solve for the top length.

$$l_T=120[ft]-2*2*10[ft]$$

$$l_T=80[ft]$$

Solution #12 (cont.)

accounts for 2:1 side slope — accounts for 2 sides

$$w_T = w_B - 2*2*h \leftarrow eq.4$$

$l_B=50[ft]$ $h=10[ft]$

Eq.4 computes the width along the top of the volume.

$$w_T = 50[ft] - 2*2*10[ft]$$

$$w_T = 10[ft]$$

Plug in the given base width and height of the volume, then solve for the top length.

$l_T=80[ft]$ $h=10[ft]$

$$V_A = l_T * w_T * h \leftarrow eq.2$$

$w_T=10[ft]$

Plug in variables l_T, w_T and h into eq.2, then solve for V_A.

$$V_A = 80[ft]*10[ft]*10[ft]$$

$$V_A = 8{,}000[ft^3]$$

Eq.5 computes volume B.

$$V_B = 0.5*l_T*h*2*h \leftarrow eq.5$$

$l_T=80[ft]$ $h=10[ft]$

Plug in the top length and height into eq.5, then solve for V_B.

$$V_B = 0.5*80[ft]*10[ft]*2*10[ft]$$

$$V_B = 8{,}000[ft]$$

Eq.6 computes volume C.

$$V_C = 0.5*w_T*h*2*h \leftarrow eq.6$$

$w_T=10[ft]$ $h=10[ft]$

Plug in the top length and height into eq.6, then solve for V_B.

$$V_C = 0.5*10[ft]*10[ft]*2*10[ft]$$

$$V_C = 1{,}000[ft]$$

Solution #12 (cont.)

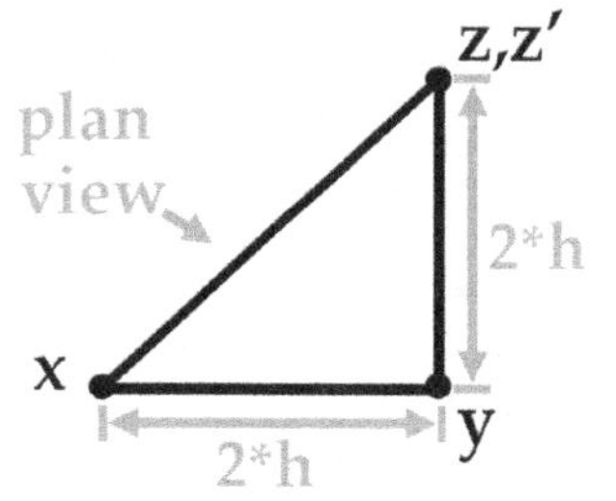

Figure 3

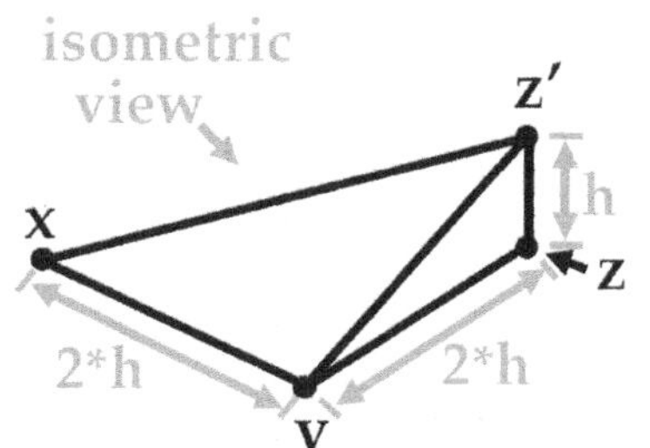

Figure 4

Figures 3 and 4 show two different views of volume D.

Points x, y, z and z′ have been added to Figures 3 and Figure 4 for reference.

area of triangle xyz — average height of triangle xyz′

$$V_D = Area_{xyz} * h_{ave,xyz'} \leftarrow eq.7$$

Eq.7 computes volume D, by multiplying the base area by the average height

h=10[ft]

$$Area_{xyz} = 0.5 * (2*h) * (2*h) \leftarrow eq.8$$

Eq.8 computes $Area_{xyz}$ as a right triangle, as shown in Figure 3.

$$Area_{xyz} = 0.5 * (2*10[ft]) * (2*10[ft])$$

$$Area_{xyz} = 200[ft^2]$$

$$h_{ave,xyz'} = (h_x + h_y + h_z)/3 \leftarrow eq.9$$

$h_x=0[ft]$ $h_y=0[ft]$ $h_z=10[ft]$

Eq.9 computes the average height of triangle xyz′.

$$h_{ave,xyz'} = (0[ft] + 0[ft] + 10[ft])/3$$

$$h_{ave,xyz'} = 3.333[ft]$$

$$V_D = Area_{xyz} * h_{ave,xyz'} \leftarrow eq.7$$

$Area_{xyz}=200[ft^2]$ $h_{ave,xyz'}=3.333[ft]$

Plug in $Area_{xyz}$ and $h_{ave,xyz'}$ into eq.7, then solve for V_D.

$$V_D = 200[ft^2] * 3.333[ft]$$

$$V_D = 667[ft^3]$$

Solution #12 (cont.)

V_A=8,000 [ft³] V_C=1,000 [ft]

$$V=V_A+2*V_B+2*V_C+8*V_D \leftarrow eq.1$$

V_B=8,000 [ft] V_D=667 [ft³]

Plug in V_A, V_B, V_C and V_D into eq.1, then solve for the volume.

$$V=8{,}000[ft^3]+2*(8{,}000[ft^3])+2*(1{,}000[ft^3])+8*(667[ft^3])$$

$$V=31{,}336[ft^3]*\frac{1[yd^3]}{27[ft^3]}$$

Convert cubic feet to cubic yards by dividing by 27 cubic feet per cubic yards.

$$V=1{,}161[yd^3]$$

Answer: A

$$V=\int_{h_1}^{h_2} l(h)*w(h)*dh \leftarrow eq.10$$

A quicker way to solve the problem is to use integration.

$$l(h)=120[ft]-4*h \leftarrow eq.11$$

Eq. 11 and eq. 12 define the length and width of the volume as a function of the height.

$$w(h)=50[ft]-4*h \leftarrow eq.12$$

In eq.10, the limits of integration are from h_1=0 [ft] to h_2=10 [ft]

h_2=10[ft] w(h)=50[ft]−4*h

$$V=\int_{h_1}^{h_2} l(h)*w(h)*dh \leftarrow eq.10$$

h_1=0[ft] l(h)=120 [ft]−4*h

Substitute in l(h), w(h), h_1 and h_2 into eq.10, then solve for V.

$$V=\int_{0[ft]}^{10[ft]}(120[ft]-4*h)*(50[ft]-4*h)*dh$$

After integrating and converting the units, the volume equals 1,160 [yd³]

$$V=1{,}160[yd^3]$$

Answer: A

Solution #13

Find: g_B ← the grade of the curve at point B

Given:

$g_1 = 1.75\%$ ← approach grade

$g_2 = -0.75\%$ ← departing grade

$Elev_A = 120.0[ft]$ ← elevation at point A

$STA_A = 12+50$
$STA_B = 14+75$
$STA_C = 18+50$
} the stationing at points A, B and C

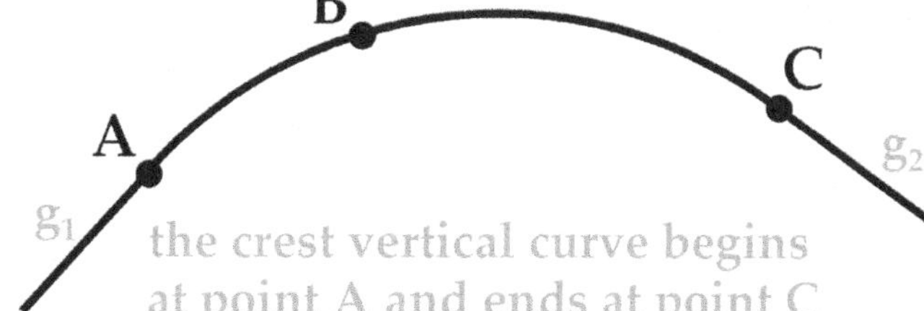

A) 0.4%
B) 0.6%
C) 0.8%
D) 1.0%

Analysis:

$$R = \frac{g_B - g_1}{L_{AB}} \quad \leftarrow eq.1$$

(g_B = grade at point B; g_1 = approach grade; R = rate of grade change; L_{AB} = length between points A and B)

Eq.1 computes the rate of grade change of the vertical curve.

$$g_B = g_1 + R * L_{AB} \quad \leftarrow eq.2$$

Solve eq.1 for g_B.

$$L_{AB} = STA_B - STA_A \quad \leftarrow eq.3$$

($STA_B = 14+75 = 1,475[ft]$; $STA_A = 12+50 = 1,250[ft]$)

Eq.3 computes the length between points A and B.

$$L_{AB} = 1,475[ft] - 1,250[ft]$$

Plug in STA_B and STA_A into eq.3, then solve for L_{AB}.

$$L_{AB} = 225[ft]$$

$$R = \frac{g_2 - g_1}{L_{AC}} \quad \leftarrow eq.4$$

(g_2 = departing grade; g_1 = approach grade; R = rate of grade change; L_{AC} = length between points A and C)

Eq.4 computes the rate of grade change based on points A and C.

Solution #13 (cont.)

$STA_C = 18+50 = 1{,}850\,[ft]$

$$L_{AC} = STA_C - STA_A \leftarrow eq.5$$

$STA_A = 12+50 = 1{,}250\,[ft]$

Eq.5 computes the length between points A and C.

$$L_{AC} = 1{,}850\,[ft] - 1{,}250\,[ft]$$

Plug in STA_C and STA_A into eq.3, then solve for L_{AC}.

$$L_{AC} = 600\,[ft]$$

$g_1 = 1.75\,\% = 0.0175$

$g_2 = -0.75\% = -0.0075$

$$R = \frac{g_2 - g_1}{L_{AC}} \leftarrow eq.4$$

$L_{AC} = 600\,[ft]$

Plug in variables g_1, g_2 and L_{AC} into eq.4, then solve for R.

$$R = \frac{-0.0075 - 0.0175}{600\,[ft]}$$

$$R = -4.167*10^{-5}\,[ft^{-1}]$$

The rate of grade change of $R = -4.167*10^{-5}\,[ft^{-1}]$ is equal to $R = -4.167*10^{-3}\,[\%/ft]$, and also equal to $R = 0.4167\,[\%/STA]$

$R = -4.167*10^{-5}\,[ft^{-1}]$

$$g_B = g_1 + R * L_{AB} \leftarrow eq.2$$

$g_1 = 0.0175$ $L_{AB} = 225\,[ft]$

Plug in variables g_1, R and L_{AB} into eq.2, then solve for g_B.

$$g_B = 0.0175 + (-4.167*10^{-5}\,[ft^{-1}]) * 225\,[ft]$$

$g_B = 0.00812$ ← grade at point B as a decimal

$g_B = 0.81\%$ ← grade at point B as a percent

Answer: C

Solution #14

Find: Q_C ← the flow rate in stream C

Given:

$T_B=20^{\circ}C$ ← the temperature of stream B

$Q_A=4.7[L/s]$ ← the flow rate in stream A

$DO_A=4.00[mg/L]$
$DO_C=5.00[mg/L]$
} the concentration of dissolved oxygen in streams A and C

no chloride present in any stream

Q_A →
Q_B →
Q_C →

stream B is saturated in dissolved oxygen

A) 2.87[L/s]
B) 5.83[L/s]
C) 6.41[L/s]
D) 7.89[L/s]

Analysis:

flow rate in streams C, A and B

$$Q_C=Q_A+Q_B \leftarrow eq.1$$

Eq. 1 computes the flow rate in stream C.

dissolved oxygen concentrations

$$DO_C=DO_A*\left(\frac{Q_A}{Q_C}\right)+DO_B*\left(\frac{Q_B}{Q_C}\right) \leftarrow eq.2$$

Eq. 2 computes the dissolved oxygen concentration in stream C as a blend of DO concentrations from stream A and stream B.

$$\left.\begin{matrix}T_B=20^{\circ}C\\ C_{Cl}=0[mg/L]\end{matrix}\right\} DO_B=9.17[mg/L]$$

Based on a temperature of 20 C, the saturated DO concentration in water equals 9.17[mg/L], in a chloride-free environment.

$Q_A=4.7[L/s]$

$$Q_B=Q_C-Q_A \leftarrow eq.3$$

$$Q_B=Q_C-4.7[L/s]$$

Solve eq. 1 for Q_B, then plug in Q_A and simplify.

$Q_B=Q_C-4.7[L/s]$

$$DO_C=DO_A*\left(\frac{Q_A}{Q_C}\right)+DO_B*\left(\frac{Q_B}{Q_C}\right) \leftarrow eq.2$$

Plug variable Q_B into eq. 2.

Solution #14 (cont.)

Plug in variables DO_A, DO_B, DO_C and Q_A into eq.4, then solve for Q_C.

DO_C=5.00[mg/L] Q_A=4.7[L/s]

$$DO_C = DO_A * \left(\frac{Q_A}{Q_C}\right) + DO_B * \left(\frac{Q_C - 4.7[L/s]}{Q_C}\right) \leftarrow eq.4$$

DO_A=4.00[mg/L] DO_B=9.17[mg/L]

$$5.00[mg/L] = 4.00[mg/L] * \left(\frac{4.7[L/s]}{Q_C}\right) + 9.17[mg/L] * \left(\frac{Q_C - 4.7[L/s]}{Q_C}\right)$$

Q_C=5.83[L/s]

<u>Answer</u>: **B**

Solution #15

Find: L ← the length of the beam

Given:

$E=2.9*10^7\,[lb/in^2]$ ← elastic modulus

$I=200\,[in^4]$ ← area moment of inertia

$y_{max}=0.17\,[in]$ ← maximum deflection in the beam

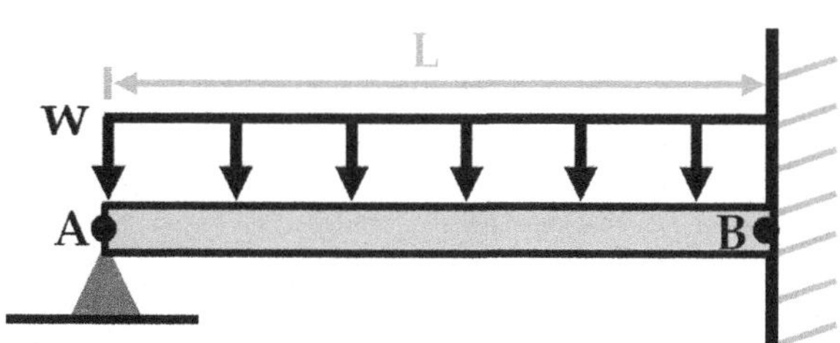

$M_B=-40{,}500\,[lb*ft]$ ← moment in the beam at point B

← propped cantilever with uniform load

A) 9 [ft]

B) 12 [ft]

C) 15 [ft]

D) 18 [ft]

Analysis:

$$y_{max}=\frac{w*L^4}{185*E*I} \quad \leftarrow eq.1$$

(w: continuous load; L: beam length; E: elastic modulus; I: area moment of inertia)

Eq.1 computes the maximum deflection in the beam

We have two equations (eq.1 and eq.2), and two unknown variables (w and L).

$$M_B=-\frac{w*L^2}{8} \quad \leftarrow eq.2$$

Eq.2 computes the moment in the beam at point B.

$M_B=-40{,}500\,[lb*ft]$

$$w=-\frac{M_B*8}{L^2} \quad \leftarrow eq.3$$

Solve eq.2 for the continuous load, w. Plug in the moment at point B, then solve for w in terms of the length, L.

$$w=-\frac{(-40{,}500\,[lb*ft])*8}{L^2}$$

$$w=324{,}000\,[lb*ft]/L^2$$

$y_{max}=0.17\,[in]$, $w=324{,}000\,[lb*ft]/L^2$

$$y_{max}=\frac{w*L^4}{185*E*I} \quad \leftarrow eq.1$$

$E=2.9*10^7\,[lb/in^2]$, $I=200\,[in^4]$

Plug in variables y_{max}, w, E and I into eq.1, then solve for L.

Solution #15 (cont.)

$$0.17[in]=\frac{(324{,}000[lb*ft]/L^2)*L^4}{185*2.9*10^7[lb/in^2]*200[in^4]}$$

$$L^2=\frac{1.8241*10^{11}[lb*in^3]}{324{,}000[lb*ft]}$$

$$L=\sqrt{5.63*10^5\left[\frac{in^3}{ft}\right]*\left(\frac{1}{12}\left[\frac{ft}{in}\right]\right)^3}$$

Convert the radicand to units of feet squared.

unit conversion factor

$$L=18.05[ft]$$

Answer: D

Solution #16

Find: P ← the axial force applied to the rod

Given:

$d_B=0.09[m]$
$d_S=0.05[m]$ } outer diameter of the brass and steel material

$E_B=1.05*10^{11}[N/m^2]$
$E_S=2.00*10^{11}[N/m^2]$ } elastic modulus of the brass and steel material

$L_o=0.644[m]$ ← initial length of rod

$\Delta L=0.002[m]$ ← change in rod length (elastic deformation)

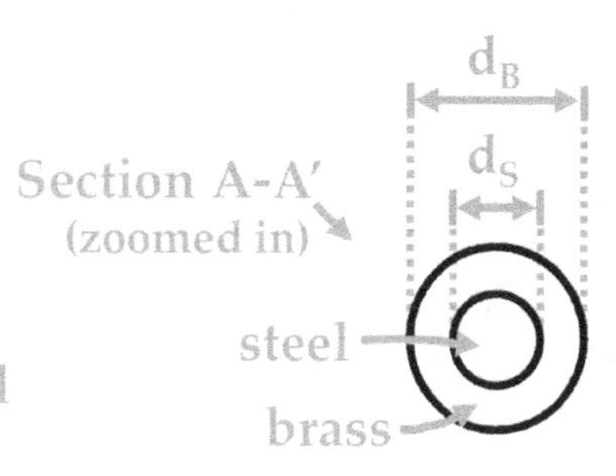

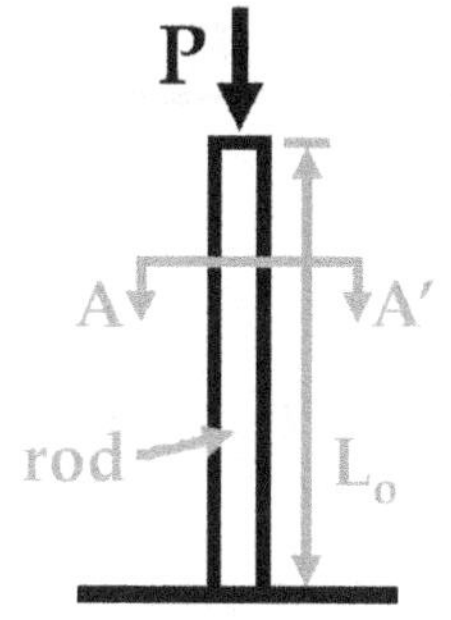

A) $1.96*10^6[N]$

B) $2.07*10^6[N]$

C) $2.65*10^6[N]$

D) $3.29*10^6[N]$

Analysis:

$$P=P_B+P_S \leftarrow eq.1$$

(total axial load; P_B, P_S: the load resisted by the brass and steel material)

Eq. 1 computes the total axial load as the sum of the axial load resisted from each material.

$$\Delta L=\frac{P*L_o}{E*A} \leftarrow eq.2$$

(ΔL: change in length; P: axial load; L_o: original length; E: elastic modulus; A: cross-sectional area)

Eq. 2 computes the change in length of a material due to axial loading.

$$P_S=\frac{\Delta L*E_S*A_S}{L_o} \leftarrow eq.3$$

Solve eq. 2 for the axial load term, P. Then add the subscript "S" to represent the steel.

$$A_S=\frac{\pi}{4}*d_S^2 \leftarrow eq.4$$

($d_S=0.05[m]$)

Eq.4 computes the area of steel based on the given diameter, d_S.

$$A_S=\frac{\pi}{4}*(0.05[m])^2$$

$$A_S=1.963*10^{-3}[m^2]$$

Solution #16 (cont.)

$E_S=2.00*10^{11}\,[N/m^2]$ $A_S=1.963*10^{-3}\,[m^2]$

$$P_S=\frac{\Delta L * E_S * A_S}{L_o} \leftarrow eq.3$$

$\Delta L=0.002\,[m]$ $L_o=0.644\,[m]$

Plug in variables ΔL, E_S, A_S and L_o into eq.3, then solve for P_S.

$$P_S=\frac{0.002[m]*2.00*10^{11}[N/m^2]*1.963*10^{-3}[m^2]}{0.644[m]}$$

$$P_S=1.219*10^{6}[N]$$

$$P_B=\frac{\Delta L * E_B * A_B}{L_o} \leftarrow eq.5$$

Eq.5 computes the axial load resisted by the brass material.

$d_B=0.09\,[m]$ $A_S=1.963*10^{-3}\,[m^2]$

$$A_B=\frac{\pi}{4} * d_B^2 - A_S \leftarrow eq.6$$

Eq.6 computes the cross-sectional area of the brass material.

$$A_B=\frac{\pi}{4} * (0.09[m])^2-1.963*10^{-3}[m^2]$$

$$A_B=4.399*10^{-3}[m^2]$$

$E_B=1.05*10^{11}\,[N/m^2]$ $A_B=4.399*10^{-3}\,[m^2]$

$$P_B=\frac{\Delta L * E_B * A_B}{L_o} \leftarrow eq.5$$

$\Delta L=0.002\,[m]$ $L_o=0.644\,[m]$

Plug in variables ΔL, E_B, A_B and L_o into eq.5, then solve for P_B.

$$P_B=\frac{0.002[m]*1.05*10^{11}[N/m^2]*4.399*10^{-3}[m^2]}{0.644[m]}$$

$$P_B=1.434*10^{6}[N]$$

Solution #16 (cont.)

$$P = P_B + P_S \leftarrow eq.1$$

$P_B = 1.434*10^6$ [N] $P_S = 1.219*10^6$ [N]

Plug in variables P_B and P_S into eq.1, then solve for P.

$$P = 1.434*10^6[N] + 1.219*10^6[N]$$

$$P = 2.653*10^6[N]$$

Answer: C

Solution #17

Find: G ← the grade of the road

Given: $v_i=100[km/hr]$ ← the initial velocity

$v_f=30[km/hr]$ ← the final velocity

$f=0.50$ ← the friction coefficient

$\Delta x=90[m]$ ← the distance the car travels while skidding from velocity v_i to velocity v_f

a negative grade refers to a downhill slope

A) -0.04
B) -0.06
C) -0.08
D) -0.10

Analysis:

$$\Delta x=\frac{v_i^2-v_f^2}{2*g*(f\pm G)} \leftarrow eq.1$$

(initial velocity v_i, final velocity v_f, gravitational acceleration g, coefficient of friction f, grade G)

Eq.1 computes the distance the car skids as is slows from velocity v_i to velocity v_f.

Solve eq.1 for G.

$$G=\frac{v_i^2-v_f^2}{2*g*\Delta x}-f \leftarrow eq.2$$

Eq.3 and eq.4 convert velocities v_i and v_f to units of meters per second

$$v_i=100\left[\frac{km}{hr}\right]*1{,}000\left[\frac{m}{km}\right]*\frac{1}{60}\left[\frac{hr}{min}\right]*\frac{1}{60}\left[\frac{min}{s}\right] \leftarrow eq.3$$

$v_i=27.78[m/s]$

$$v_i=30\left[\frac{km}{hr}\right]*1{,}000\left[\frac{m}{km}\right]*\frac{1}{60}\left[\frac{hr}{min}\right]*\frac{1}{60}\left[\frac{min}{s}\right] \leftarrow eq.4$$

$v_i=8.33[m/s]$

Solution #17 (cont.)

v_i=27.78 [m/s] v_f=8.33 [m/s]

$$G=\frac{v_i^2-v_f^2}{2*g*\Delta x}-f \quad \leftarrow eq.2$$

f=0.50

g=9.81 [m/s²] Δx=90 [m]

Plug in variables v_i, v_f, g, f and Δx into eq. 2, then solve for G.

$$G=\frac{(27.78\,[m/s])^2-(8.33\,[m/s])^2}{2*9.81[m/s]*90\,[m]}-0.50$$

$$G=-0.102$$

The calculated grade of -0.102 is most nearly -0.10.

Answer: D

Solution #18

Find: Air Content ← the percent air content in the concrete mix

Given:

Material	SG	Weight [lb]
Cement	3.15	658
Fine Aggregate	2.63	1,211
Coarse Aggregate	2.71	1,742
Water	1.00	260
Air	-	0

$\gamma_W = 62.4 [lb/ft^3]$ ← unit weight of water

$V_T = 27.00 [ft^3]$ ← total volume of the concrete mix

A) 1.8%

B) 2.2%

C) 6.7%

D) 7.1%

Analysis:

$$\text{Air Content} = \frac{V_A}{V_T} \leftarrow eq.1$$

V_A = volume of air; V_T = total volume

Eq.1 computes the percent of air content in the concrete mix.

$$V_A = V_T - V_C - V_{FA} - V_{CA} - V_W \leftarrow eq.2$$

V_T = total volume; V_C = volume of cement; V_{FA} = volume of fine aggregate; V_{CA} = volume of coarse aggregate; V_W = volume of water

Eq.2 computes volume of air by subtracting the volume of the other mix materials from the total volume

$$V_C = \frac{W_C}{\gamma_C} \leftarrow eq.3$$

W_C = weight of cement; γ_C = unit weight of cement

Eq.3 computes the volume of cement.

$$\gamma_C = SG_C * \gamma_W \leftarrow eq.4$$

$SG_C = 3.15$; $\gamma_W = 62.4 [lb/ft^3]$

Eq.4 computes the unit weight of cement by multiplying the specific gravity of the cement by the unit weight of water.

$$\gamma_C = 3.15 * 62.4 [lb/ft^3]$$

$$\gamma_C = 195.56 [lb/ft^3]$$

Solution #18 (cont.)

$W_C = 658\,[lb]$

$$V_C = \frac{W_C}{\gamma_C} \leftarrow eq.3$$

$\gamma_C = 196.56\,[lb/ft^3]$

Plug in W_C and γ_C into eq. 3, then solve for the volume of cement, V_C.

$$V_C = \frac{658\,[lb]}{196.56\,[lb/ft^3]}$$

$$V_C = 3.35\,[ft^3]$$

$$V_{FA} = \frac{W_{FA}}{\gamma_{FA}} \leftarrow eq.5$$

weight of the fine aggregate (W_{FA}); unit weight of the fine aggregate (γ_{FA})

Eq. 5 computes the volume of fine aggregate.

$$\gamma_{FA} = SG_{FA} * \gamma_W \leftarrow eq.6$$

$SG_{FA} = 2.63$ $\quad$ $\gamma_W = 62.4\,[lb/ft^3]$

Eq. 6 computes the unit weight of the fine aggregate by multiplying the specific gravity of the fine aggregate by the unit weight of water.

$$\gamma_{FA} = 2.63 * 62.4\,[lb/ft^3]$$

$$\gamma_{FA} = 164.11\,[lb/ft^3]$$

$W_{FA} = 1{,}211\,[lb]$

$$V_{FA} = \frac{W_{FA}}{\gamma_{FA}} \leftarrow eq.5$$

$\gamma_{FA} = 164.11\,[lb/ft^3]$

Plug in W_{FA} and γ_{FA} into eq. 5, then solve for the volume of fine aggregate, V_{FA}.

$$V_{FA} = \frac{1{,}211\,[lb]}{164.11\,[lb/ft^3]}$$

Solution #18 (cont.)

$$V_{FA}=7.38[ft^3]$$

$$V_{CA}=\frac{W_{CA}}{\gamma_{CA}} \leftarrow eq.7$$

weight of the coarse aggregate (W_{CA}); unit weight of the coarse aggregate (γ_{CA})

Eq.7 computes the volume of coarse aggregate.

$$\gamma_{CA}=SG_{CA}*\gamma_W \leftarrow eq.8$$

$SG_{CA}=2.71$ $\quad\gamma_W=62.4[lb/ft^3]$

Eq.8 computes the unit weight of the coarse aggregate by multiplying the specific gravity of the coarse aggregate by the unit weight of water.

$$\gamma_{CA}=2.71*62.4[lb/ft^3]$$

$$\gamma_{CA}=169.10[lb/ft^3]$$

$W_{CA}=1{,}742[lb]$

$$V_{CA}=\frac{W_{CA}}{\gamma_{CA}} \leftarrow eq.7$$

$\gamma_{CA}=169.10[lb/ft^3]$

Plug in W_{FA} and γ_{FA} into eq.7, then solve for the volume of fine aggregate, V_{FA}.

$$V_{CA}=\frac{1{,}742[lb]}{169.10[lb/ft^3]}$$

$$V_{CA}=10.30[ft^3]$$

$W_W=260[lb]$

$$V_W=\frac{W_W}{\gamma_W} \leftarrow eq.9$$

$\gamma_W=62.4[lb/ft^3]$

Eq.9 computes the volume of water, using the weight of water and unit weight of water.

$$V_W=\frac{260[lb]}{62.4[lb/ft^3]}$$

Solution #18 (cont.)

$$V_W = 4.17\,[ft^3]$$

$V_T = 27.00\,[ft^3]$ $V_{CA} = 10.30\,[ft^3]$

$$V_A = V_T - V_C - V_{FA} - V_{CA} - V_W \leftarrow eq.2$$

$V_C = 3.35\,[ft^3]$ $V_{FA} = 7.38\,[ft^3]$ $V_W = 4.17\,[ft^3]$

Plug in variables V_T, V_C, V_{FA}, V_{CA} and V_W into eq.2, then solve for V_A

$$V_A = 27.00\,[ft^3] - 3.35\,[ft^3] - 7.38\,[ft^3] - 10.30\,[ft^3] - 4.17\,[ft^3]$$

$$V_A = 1.80\,[ft^3]$$

$V_A = 1.80\,[ft^3]$

$$\text{Air Content} = \frac{V_A}{V_T} \leftarrow eq.1$$

$V_A = 27.00\,[ft^3]$

Plug in variables V_A and V_T into eq. 1, then solve for the air content.

$$\text{Air Content} = \frac{1.80\,[ft^3]}{27.00\,[ft^3]}$$

$$\text{Air Content} = 0.0667$$

Convert the decimal to a percent by multiplying by 100%

$$\text{Air Content} = 6.67\%$$

Answer: C

6.67% air content is most nearly 6.7%.

Solution #19

Find: Soil Classification

Given:

Fine-grained soil

PL=37% ← plastic limit of the soil

liquid limit test data

Test	N (the number of drops)	w (water content)
A	18	60%
B	21	54%
C	35	35%

A) CL
B) CH
C) ML
D) MH

Analysis:

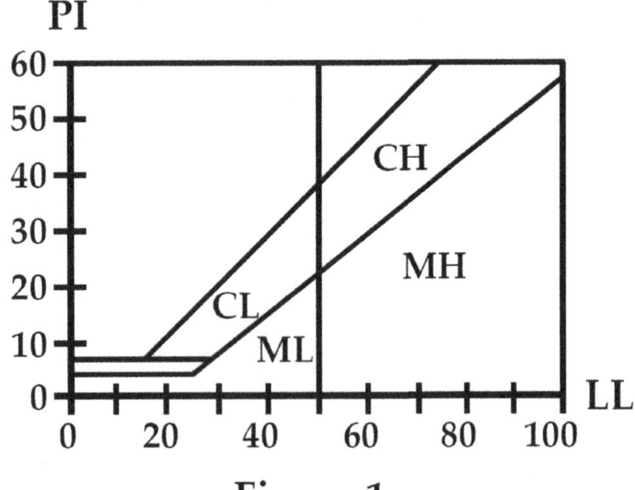

Figure 1

Plot the Liquid Limit (LL) and Plasticity Index (PI) on the Casagrande Plasticity Chart (Figure 1) to determine the soil classification.

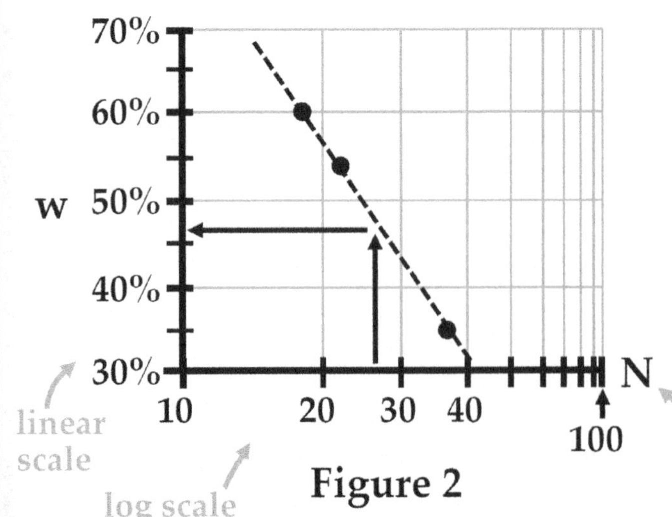

Figure 2

The liquid limit of the soil is determined using the test data.

In Figure 2, we plot the water content against the number of turns, then sketch a best-fit line through the three points. The liquid limit is the water content predicted by the best-fit line for N=25.

Solution #19 (cont.)

$$LL = 47\%$$

From Figure 2, we notice the liquid limit of the soil equals 47%.

$$PI = LL - PL \leftarrow eq.1$$

PL=47% LL=37%

Eq.1 computes the plasticity index (PI) of the soil as the liquid limit (LL) minus the plastic limit (PL).

$$PI = 47\% - 37\%$$

$$PI = 10\%$$

Plug in variables LL and PL into eq.1, then solve for PI.

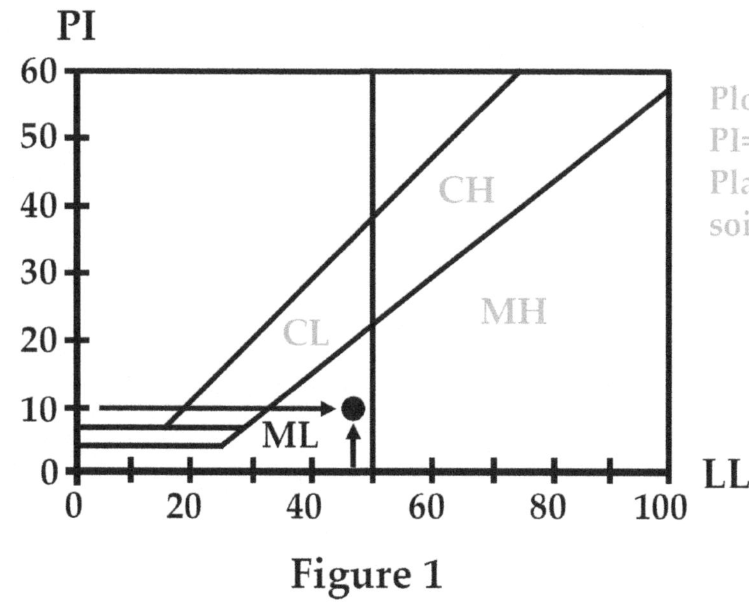

Figure 1

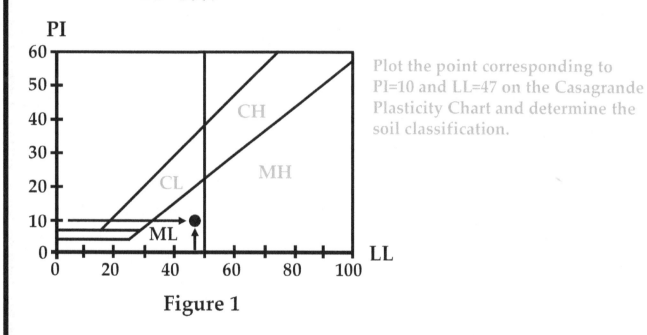

Plot the point corresponding to PI=10 and LL=47 on the Casagrande Plasticity Chart and determine the soil classification.

Answer: C

The soil classifies as a low-plasticity silt, ML.

Solution #20

Find: L ← superelevation runoff

Given:

$f_s=0.16$ ← coefficient of static friction

SRR=1:300 ← transition rate

v=40[mi/hr] ← velocity

w=12[ft] ← lane width

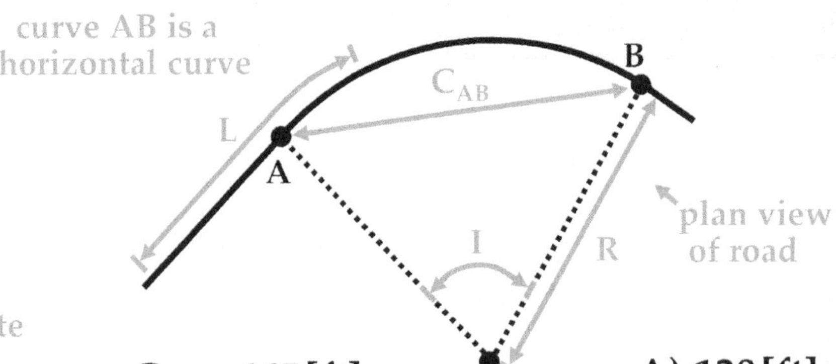

$C_{AB}=465$[ft] ← chord length

I=60° ← interior angle

A) 120[ft]

B) 170[ft]

C) 210[ft]

D) 250[ft]

Analysis:

$$L=\frac{w*e}{SRR} \leftarrow eq.1$$

(w: lane width; e: superelevation rate; SRR: transition rate)

Eq.1 computes the superelevation runoff based on the lane width, superelevation rate and the superelevation runout rate (transition rate).

$$e=\frac{v^2}{g*R}-f_s \leftarrow eq.2$$

(v: velocity; f_s: static friction coefficient; g: gravitational acceleration; R: curve radius)

Eq.2 computes the superelevation rate.

$$C_{AB}=2*R*\sin(I/2) \leftarrow eq.3$$

Eq.3 relates the chord length of curve AB to the radius and interior angle of the horizontal curve.

$$R=\frac{C_{AB}}{2*\sin(I/2)} \leftarrow eq.4$$

(C_{AB}=465[ft]; I=60°)

Solve eq.3 for the radius, then plug in C_{AB} and I, then solve for R.

$$R=\frac{465[ft]}{2*\sin(60°/2)}$$

When the interior angle of a curve is 60°, the chord length equals the radius.

Solution #20 (cont.)

$$R=465\,[ft]$$

$$v=40\left[\frac{mi}{hr}\right]*5{,}280\left[\frac{ft}{mi}\right]*\frac{1}{60}\left[\frac{hr}{min}\right]*\frac{1}{60}\left[\frac{min}{s}\right] \leftarrow eq.5$$

Eq. 5 converts the velocity to units of feet per second

$$v=58.67\,[ft/s]$$

v=58.67 [ft/s]; $f_s=0.16$; g=32.2 [ft/s²]; R=465 [ft]

$$e=\frac{v^2}{g*R}-f_s \leftarrow eq.2$$

Plug in variables v, g, R and f_s into eq. 2, then solve for e.

$$e=\frac{(58.67\,[ft/s])^2}{32.2[ft/s^2]*465\,[ft]}-0.16$$

$$e=0.0698$$

w=12 [ft]; e=0.0698; SRR=(1/300)

$$L=\frac{w*e}{SRR} \leftarrow eq.1$$

Plug in variables w, e, and SRR into eq. 1 then solve for L.

$$L=\frac{12[ft]*0.0698}{(1/300)}$$

$$L=251.3\,[ft]$$

Answer: D

Solution #21

Find: I ← the area moment of inertia about the x axis

Given:

$h_f = 2[in]$ ← the height of the flange

$h_w = 8[in]$ ← the height of the web

$w_f = 8[in]$ ← the width of the flange

$w_w = 2[in]$ ← the width of the web

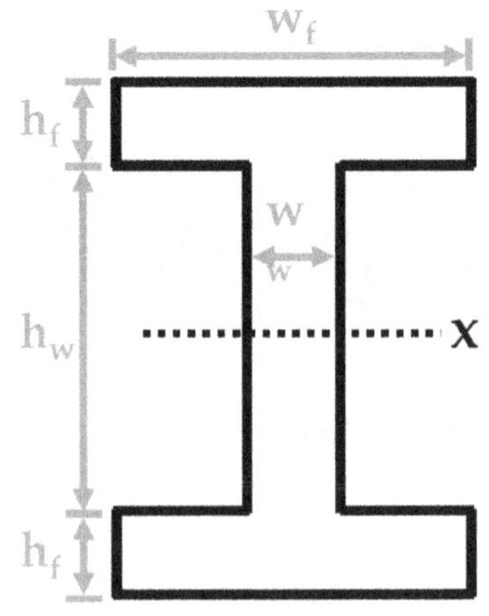

A) 405 [in⁴]

B) 490 [in⁴]

C) 810 [in⁴]

D) 890 [in⁴]

Analysis:

$$I = I_A + I_B + I_C \leftarrow eq.1$$

(I: area moment of inertia)

Eq.1 computes the area moment of inertia by summing up the area moment of inertia values of three parts A, B and C.

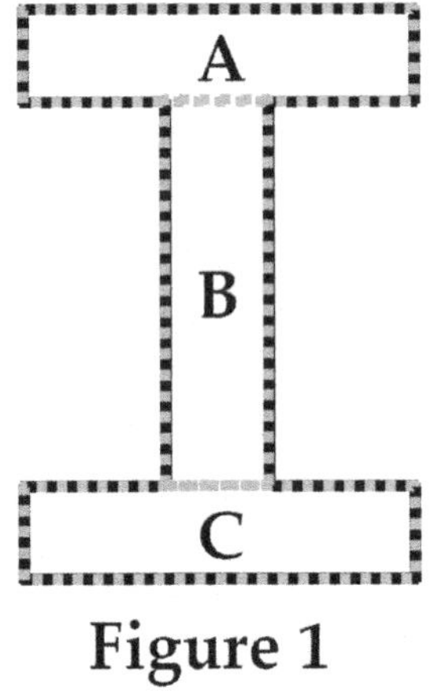

Figure 1

Figure 1 shows the cross-section divided into parts A, B and C.

Use the parallel axis theorem to compute the individual area moment of inertia values.

Eq.2 computes the area moment of inertia for part A.

$$I_A = I_{A,C} + A_A * d_A^2 \leftarrow eq.2$$

$I_{A,C}$: centroidal area moment of inertia of part A; A_A: area of part A; d_A: distance between the centroid of part A and the centroid of entire cross-section.

The distance d_A is measured perpendicular to the x axis.

$$I_{A,C} = I_{C,C} = \frac{w_f * h_f^3}{12} \leftarrow eq.3$$

($w_f = 8[in]$, $h_f = 2[in]$)

Eq.3 computes the centroidal area moment of inertia of parts A and C, based on variables w_f and h_f.

Solution #21 (cont.)

$$I_{A,C}=I_{C,C}=\frac{8[in]*(2[in])^3}{12}$$

$$I_{A,C}=I_{C,C}=5.333[in^4]$$

$w_f=8[in]$ $h_f=2[in]$

$$A_A=A_C=w_f*h_f \leftarrow eq.4$$

Eq.4 computes the area of parts A and C.

$$A_A=A_C=8[in]*2[in]$$

$$A_A=A_C=16[in^2]$$

$$d_A=y_A-y_o \leftarrow eq.5$$

Eq.5 computes the distance d_A.

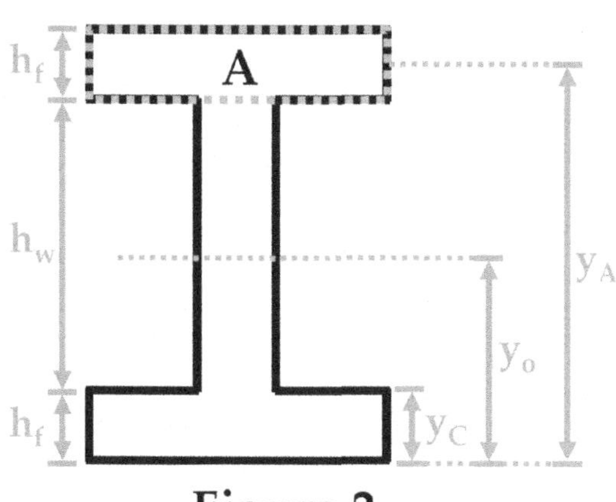

Figure 2

Figure 2 identifies distances y_o, y_A, and y_c.

y_A is the distance from the bottom of the cross-section to the centroid of part A.

y_o is the distance from the bottom of the cross-section to the x-axis.

$h_f=2[in]$ $h_w=8[in]$

$$y_o=h_f+0.5*h_w \leftarrow eq.6$$

Eq.6 computes the height to the x-axis.

$$y_o=2[in]+0.5*8[in]$$

$$y_o=6[in]$$

Solution #21 (cont.)

$h_w=8[in]$

$$y_A=h_f+h_w+0.5*h_f \leftarrow eq.7$$

$h_f=2[in]$

Eq.7 computes the height to the centroid of part A.

$$y_A=2[in]+8[in]+0.5*2[in]$$

$$y_A=11[in]$$

$y_A=11[in]$ $y_o=6[in]$

$$d_A=y_A-y_o \leftarrow eq.5$$

Plug in variables y_A and y_o into eq.5, then solve for d_A.

$$d_A=11[in]-6[in]$$

$$d_A=5[in]$$

$A_A=16[in^2]$

$$I_A=I_{A,C}+A_A*d_A^2 \leftarrow eq.2$$

$I_{A,C}=5.333[in^4]$ $d_A=5[in]$

Plug in variables $I_{A,C}$, A_A and d_A into eq.2, then solve for I_A.

$$I_A=5.333[in^4]+16[in^2]*(5[in])^2$$

$$I_A=405.3[in^4]$$

$$I_B=I_{B,C}+A_B*d_B^2 \leftarrow eq.8$$

Eq.8 computes the area moment of inertia for part B.

$w_w=2[in]$ $h_w=8[in]$

$$I_{B,C}=\frac{w_w*h_w^3}{12} \leftarrow eq.9$$

Eq.9 computes the centroidal area moment of inertia of part B based on variables w_w and h_w.

Solution #21 (cont.)

$$I_{B,C}=\frac{2[in]*(8[in])^3}{12}$$

$$I_{B,C}=85.33[in^4]$$

$w_w=2[in]$ $h_w=8[in]$

$$A_B=w_w*h_w \leftarrow eq.10$$

Eq. 10 computes the area of part B.

$$A_B=2[in]*8[in]$$

$$A_B=16[in^2]$$

$$d_B=0[in^2]$$

The distance d_B equals 0 because the centroid of part B coincides with the centroid of the entire cross-section.

$A_B=16[in^2]$

$$I_B=I_{B,C}+A_B*d_B^2 \leftarrow eq.8$$

$I_{B,C}=85.33[in^4]$ $d_B=0[in]$

Plug in variables $I_{B,C}$, A_B and d_B into eq. 8, then solve for I_B.

$$I_B=85.33[in^4]+16[in^2]*(0[in])^2$$

$$I_B=85.33[in^4]$$

$$I_C=I_{C,C}+A_C*d_C^2 \leftarrow eq.11$$

Eq.11 computes the area moment of inertia for part C.

$$d_C=y_o-y_C \leftarrow eq.12$$

Eq. 12 computes the distance d_C.

$$y_C=0.5*h_f \leftarrow eq.13$$

$h_f=2[in]$

Eq. 13 computes the height to the centroid of part C.

Solution #21 (cont.)

$$y_C=0.5*2[in]$$

$$y_C=1[in]$$

$y_o=6[in]$ $y_C=1[in]$

$$d_C=y_o-y_C \leftarrow eq. 12$$

Plug in variables y_o and y_C into eq. 12, then solve for d_C.

$$d_C=6[in]-1[in]$$

$$d_C=5[in]$$

$A_C=16[in^2]$

$$I_C=I_{C,C}+A_C*d_C^2 \leftarrow eq. 11$$

$I_{C,C}=5.333[in^4]$ $d_C=5[in]$

Plug in variables $I_{C,C}$, A_C and d_C into eq. 11, then solve for I_C.

$$I_A=5.333[in^4]+16[in^2]*(5[in])^2$$

$$I_A=405.3[in^4]$$

$I_A=405.3[in^4]$ $I_C=405.3[in^4]$

$$I=I_A+I_B+I_C \leftarrow eq. 1$$

$I_B=85.33[in^4]$

Plug in variables I_A, I_B and I_C into eq. 1, then solve for I.

$$I=405.3[in^4]+85.33[in^4]+405.3[in^4]$$

$$I=896[in^4]$$

Answer: D

Solution #22

Find: W_{haul} ← the weight of extra soil needed to be hauled off site after the terrain is leveled to elevation=0[ft]

Given: w=30[ft] ← width of cut pile and fill pit (into and out of the page)

γ_T=120[lb/ft^3] ← the total unit weight of the soil

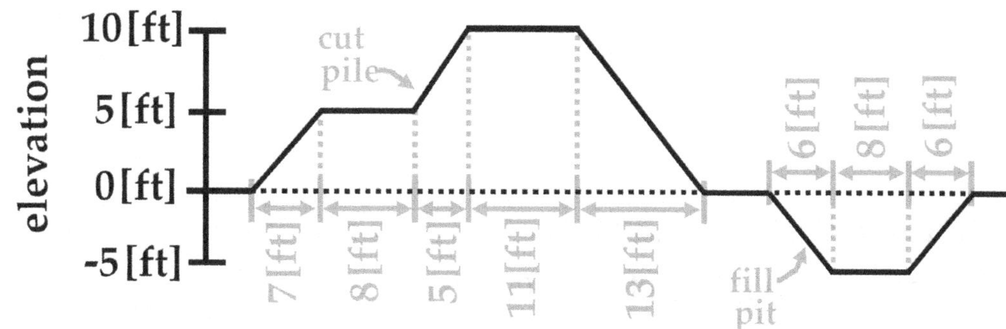

A) 120[ton]

B) 240[ton]

C) 360[ton]

D) 480[ton]

Analysis:

$$W_{haul}=\gamma_T * V_{haul} \leftarrow eq.1$$

total unit weight of soil; volume of soil to be hauled

Eq.1 computes the weight of the soil to be hauled off site.

$$V_{hual}=w*(A_{cut}-A_{fill}) \leftarrow eq.2$$

width of cut pile and fill pit; cross-sectional area of cut pile and fill pit

Eq.2 computes the volume of soil to be hauled off site.

Figure 1 subdivides the cut and fill areas into smaller sub-areas

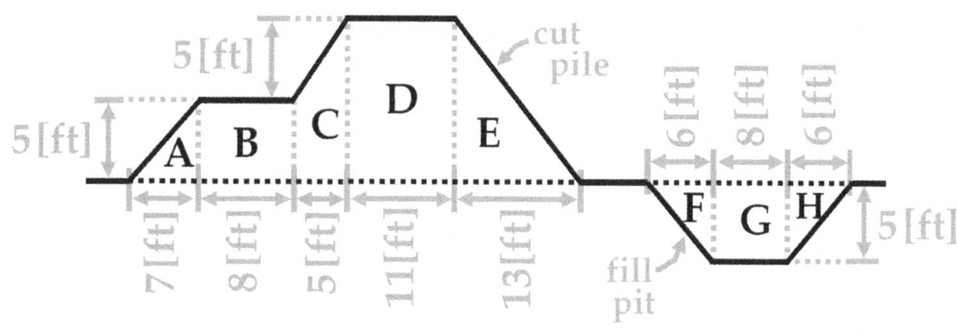

Figure 1

$$A_{cut}=A_A+A_B+A_C+A_D+A_E \leftarrow eq.3$$

Eq.3 computes the cross-sectional area of the cut pile.

Solution #22 (cont.)

$A_A=7[ft]*(0.5*(0[ft]+5[ft]))$

$A_D=11[ft]*10[ft]$

$$A_{cut}=A_A+A_B+A_C+A_D+A_E \leftarrow eq.3$$

$A_B=8[ft]*5[ft]$

$A_E=13[ft]*(0.5*(10[ft]+0[ft]))$

$A_C=5[ft]*(0.5*(5[ft]+10[ft]))$

Plug in the values for variables A_A, A_B, A_C, A_D and A_E into eq.3, then solve for the cut area.

$$A_{cut}=7[ft]*(0.5*(0[ft]+5[ft]))+8[ft]*5[ft]$$
$$+5[ft]*(0.5*(5[ft]+10[ft]))+11[ft]*10[ft]$$
$$+13[ft]*(0.5*(10[ft]+0[ft]))$$

$$A_{cut}=270[ft^2]$$

$$A_{cut}=A_E+A_F+A_G \leftarrow eq.4$$

Eq.4 computes the cross-sectional area of the fill pit.

$A_H=6[ft]*(0.5*(0[ft]+5[ft]))$

$A_G=8[ft]*5[ft]$

$$A_{cut}=A_F+A_G+A_H \leftarrow eq.4$$

$A_F=6[ft]*(0.5*(0[ft]+5[ft]))$

Plug in the equations for A_F, A_G, and A_H into eq.4, then solve for the fill area.

$$A_{fill}=6[ft]*(0.5*(0[ft]+5[ft]))+8[ft]*5[ft]+6[ft]*(0.5*(0[ft]+5[ft]))$$

$$A_{fill}=70[ft^2]$$

$A_{cut}=270[ft^2]$

$$V_{hual}=w*(A_{cut}-A_{fill}) \leftarrow eq.2$$

$w=30[ft]$ $A_{fill}=70[ft^2]$

Plug in variables w, A_{cut} and A_{fill} into eq.2, then solve for V_{hual}.

$$V_{hual}=30[ft]*(270[ft^2]-70[ft^2])$$

Solution #22 (cont.)

$$V_{haul}=6{,}000\,[ft^3]$$

$$W_{haul}=\gamma_T * V_{haul} \leftarrow eq.1$$

$\gamma_T=120\,[lb/ft^3]$ $V_{haul}=6{,}000\,[ft^3]$

Plug in variables γ_T and V_{haul} into eq. 1, then solve for W_{haul}.

$$W_{haul}=120\,[lb/ft^3]*6{,}000\,[ft^3]$$

Convert pounds to tons by dividing by 2,000 pounds per ton.

$$W_{haul}=720{,}000\,[lb]*\frac{1\,[ton]}{2{,}000\,[lb]}$$

$$W_{haul}=360\,[ton]$$

<u>Answer</u>: C

Solution #23

Find: σ_h @ $d=12[ft]$ ← the horizontal stress at a depth of 12 feet

$d_{gw}=4[ft]$ ← depth to the groundwater table

Given:

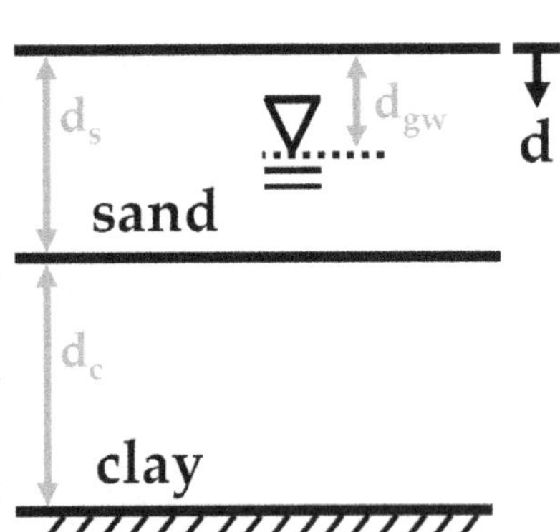

$K_{o,s}=0.45$
$K_{o,c}=0.65$
} at-rest lateral earth pressure coefficients for the sand and clay layers

$d_s=8[ft]$
$d_c=9[ft]$
} thickness of the sand and clay layers

$\gamma_{T,s}=120[lb/ft^3]$
$\gamma_{T,c}=100[lb/ft^3]$
} unit weights of the sand and clay layers

A) $890[lb/ft^2]$
B) $1,010[lb/ft^2]$
C) $1,060[lb/ft^2]$
D) $1,150[lb/ft^2]$

Analysis:

$$\sigma_{h,12}=\sigma'_{h,12}+u_{12} \quad \leftarrow eq.1$$

($\sigma_{h,12}$: total horizontal stress; $\sigma'_{h,12}$: effective horizontal stress; u_{12}: pore-water pressure)

Eq.1 computes the total horizontal stress at a depth of 12 feet.

$$u_{12}=\gamma_W{}^*d_u \quad \leftarrow eq.2$$

(γ_W: unit weight of water; d_u: depth beneath the groundwater table)

Eq.2 computes the pore-water pressure at a depth of 12 feet.

$d=12[ft]$ $\quad d_{gw}=4[ft]$

$$d_u=d-d_{gw} \quad \leftarrow eq.3$$

Eq.3 computes the depth of the point of interest beneath the groundwater table.

$$d_u=12[ft]-4[ft]$$

$$d_u=8[ft]$$

Plug in variables d and d_{gw} into eq.3, then solve for d_u.

$d_u=8[ft]$

$$u_{12}=\gamma_W{}^*d_u \quad \leftarrow eq.2$$

$\gamma_W=62.4[lb/ft^3]$

Plug in variables γ_W and d_u into eq.2, then solve for u_{12}.

Solution #23 (cont.)

$$u_{12}=62.4[lb/ft^3]*8[ft]$$

$$u_{12}=499[lb/ft^2]$$

$$\sigma'_{h,12}=\sigma'_{v,12}*K_{o,c} \leftarrow eq.4$$

effective vertical stress; at-rest lateral earth pressure coefficient

Eq. 4 computes the effective horizontal stress at a depth of 12 feet.

$$\sigma'_{v,12}=\sigma_{v,12}-u_{12} \leftarrow eq.5$$

total vertical stress; pore-water pressure

Eq. 5 computes the effective vertical stress at a depth of 12 feet.

unit weight of the sand layer; unit weight of the clay layer

$$\sigma_{v,12}=\gamma_s*d_s+\gamma_c*d_{c,i} \leftarrow eq.6$$

thickenss of the sand layer; depth to the point of interest in the clay layer

Eq. 6 computes the total vertical stress at a depth of 12 feet.

$d=12[ft]$ $d_s=8[ft]$

$$d_{c,i}=d-d_s \leftarrow eq.7$$

Eq. 7 computes the depth of our point of interest beneath the sand-clay interface.

$$d_{c,i}=12[ft]-8[ft]$$

$$d_{c,i}=4[ft]$$

Plug in variables d and ds into eq. 7, then solve for $d_{c,i}$.

$\gamma_s=120[lb/ft^3]$ $\gamma_c=100[lb/ft^3]$

$$\sigma_{v,12}=\gamma_s*d_s+\gamma_c*d_{c,i} \leftarrow eq.6$$

$d_s=8[ft]$ $d_{c,i}=4[ft]$

Plug in γ_s, d_s, γ_c and $d_{c,i}$ into eq. 6, then solve for $\sigma_{v,12}$.

$$\sigma_{v,12}=120[lb/ft^3]*8[ft]+100[lb/ft^3]*4[ft]$$

Solution #23 (cont.)

$$\sigma_{v,12}=1{,}360\,[lb/ft^2]$$

$\sigma_{v,12}=1{,}360\,[lb/ft^2]$ $u_{12}=499\,[lb/ft^2]$

$$\sigma'_{v,12}=\sigma_{v,12}-u_{12} \leftarrow eq.5$$

Plug in $\sigma_{v,12}$ and u_{12} into eq. 5, then solve for $\sigma'_{v,12}$.

$$\sigma'_{v,12}=1{,}360\,[lb/ft^2]-499\,[lb/ft^2]$$

$$\sigma'_{v,12}=861\,[lb/ft^2]$$

$\sigma'_{v,12}=861\,[lb/ft^2]$

$$\sigma'_{h,12}=\sigma'_{v,12}*K_{o,c} \leftarrow eq.4$$

$K_{o,c}=0.65$

Plug in $\sigma'_{v,12}$ and $K_{o,c}$ into eq. 4, then solve for $\sigma'_{h,12}$.

$$\sigma'_{h,12}=861\,[lb/ft^2]*0.65$$

$$\sigma'_{h,12}=560\,[lb/ft^2]$$

$u_{12}=499\,[lb/ft^2]$

$$\sigma_{h,12}=\sigma'_{h,12}+u_{12} \leftarrow eq.1$$

$\sigma'_{h,12}=560\,[lb/ft^2]$

Plug in $\sigma'_{h,12}$ and u_{12} into eq. 1, then solve for $\sigma_{h,12}$.

$$\sigma_{h,12}=560\,[lb/ft^2]+499\,[lb/ft^2]$$

$$\sigma_{h,12}=1{,}059\,[lb/ft^2]$$

<u>Answer</u>: **C**

Solution #24

Find: $y_{x=3[ft]}$ ← the deflection of the beam 3 feet from the end

Given:

$E=2.9*10^7[lb/in^2]$ ← elastic modulus

$I=6,000[in^4]$ ← area moment of inertia

$k=3.3564*10^7[lb/ft]$ ← stiffness of the beam

$P_B=4,000[k]$ ← point load at mid-span

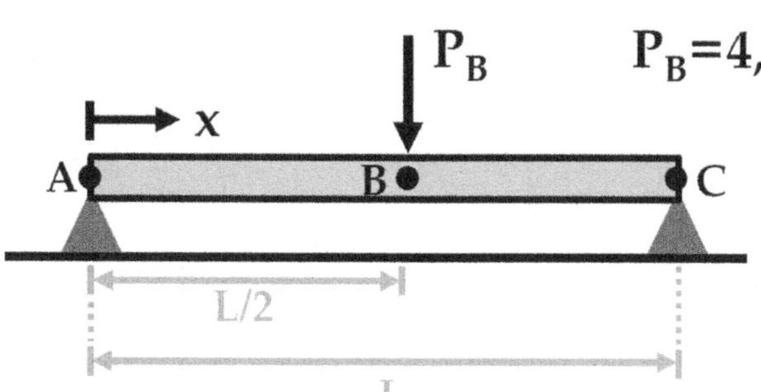

← simply supported beam with a point load P_B

A) 1[in]

B) 2[in]

C) 3[in]

D) 4[in]

Analysis:

Eq. 1 computes the displacement at x=3 feet due to point load P_B.

$$y_{x=3[ft]}=\left(\frac{P_B}{48*E*I}\right)*(3*x*L^2-4*x^3) \quad \leftarrow eq.1$$

(P_B: point load at point B; L: beam length; E: elastic modulus; I: area moment of inertia; x: distance from from point A)

Eq.2 computes the beam stiffness.

$$k=\frac{48*E*I}{L^3} \quad \leftarrow eq.2$$

(k: stiffness; L: beam length; E: elastic modulus; I: area moment of inertia)

Solve eq. 2 for the beam length.

$$L=\left(\frac{48*E*I}{k}\right)^{1/3} \quad \leftarrow eq.3$$

Eq.4 converts the stiffness to units of pounds per inch.

$$k=3.3564*10^7\left[\frac{lb}{ft}\right]*\left(\frac{1}{12}\left[\frac{ft}{in}\right]\right)=2.797*10^6\left[\frac{lb}{in}\right] \quad \leftarrow eq.4$$

Plug in variables E, I and k into eq. 3, then solve for L.

$$L=\left(\frac{48*E*I}{k}\right)^{1/3} \quad \leftarrow eq.3$$

($E=2.9*10^7[lb/in^2]$; $I=6,000[in^4]$; $k=2.797*10^6[lb/in]$)

Solution #24 (cont.)

$$L=\left(\frac{48*2.9*10^7[lb/in^2]*6{,}000[in^4]}{2.797*10^6[lb/in]}\right)^{1/3}$$

$$L=144[in]*\frac{1}{12}\left[\frac{ft}{in}\right]=12[ft] \leftarrow eq.5$$

Eq. 5 converts the beam length to units of feet.

$$P_B=4{,}000[k]*1{,}000\left[\frac{lb}{k}\right]=4*10^6[lb] \leftarrow eq.6$$

Eq. 6 converts the point load to units of pounds.

$P_B=4*10^6[lb]$; $L=12[ft]$

$$y_{x=3[ft]}=\left(\frac{P_B}{48*E*I}\right)*(3*x*L^2-4*x^3) \leftarrow eq.1$$

$E=2.9*10^7[lb/in^2]$; $I=6{,}000[in^4]$; $x=3[ft]$

Plug in variables P_B, E, I, x and L into eq. 1, then solve for the deflection at x=3.

$$y_{x=3[ft]}=\left(\frac{4*10^6[lb]}{48*2.9*10^7[lb/in^2]*6{,}000[in^4]}\right)*\left(3*3[ft]*(12[ft])^2-4*(3[ft])^3\right)$$

$$y_{x=3[ft]}=5.690*10^{-4}\left[\frac{ft^3}{in^2}\right]*\left(12\left[\frac{in}{ft}\right]\right)^3 \leftarrow eq.7$$

Eq. 7 converts the deflection to units of inches.

$$y_{x=3[ft]}=0.983[in]$$

Answer: A

Solution #25

Find: v_D ← the design speed of the curve

Given:

R=500[ft] ← curve radius

C=350[ft] ← chord length

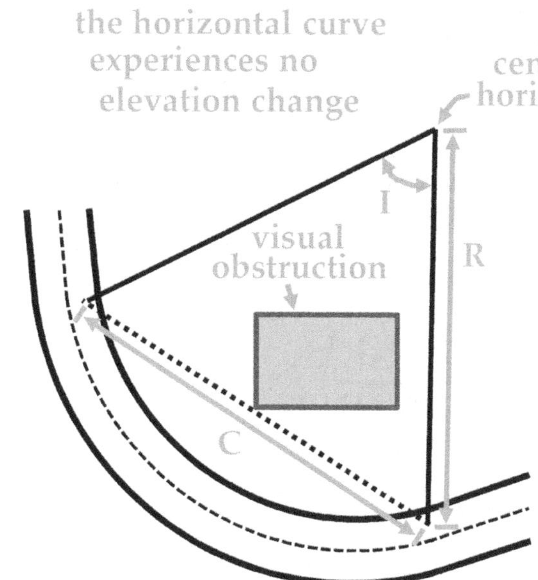

A) 40[mph]
B) 50[mph]
C) 60[mph]
D) 70[mph]

Analysis:

$$S \geq S_{min} \quad \leftarrow ieq.1$$

S: stopping sight distance; S_{min}: minimum stopping sight distance

Ieq.1 states the sight distance of the curve must be at least the minimum stopping sight distance.

The minimum stopping sight distance of the curve depends on the design speed.

design speeds		minimum stopping sight distances
A) 40[mph]	→	305[ft]
B) 50[mph]	→	425[ft]
C) 60[mph]	→	570[ft]
D) 70[mph]	→	730[ft]

Figure 1

Figure 1 shows AASHTO minimum stopping sight distances based on the four given design speeds.

$$S = \frac{\pi * R * I}{180^{\circ}} \quad \leftarrow eq.1$$

S: stopping sight distance; R: curve radius; I: interior angle (in degrees)

Eq.1 computes the stopping sight distance, S, based on the geometry of the curve.

The stopping sight distance is the length along the curve connecting the minimum line of sight.

$$C = 2 * R * \sin(I/2) \quad \leftarrow eq.2$$

C: chord length; R: curve radius; I: interior angle

Eq.2 computes chord length as a function of the curve radius and interior angle.

Solution #25 (cont.)

C=350[ft], R=500[ft]

$$I=2*\sin^{-1}\left(\frac{C}{2*R}\right)$$

Solve eq. 2 for the interior angle, then plug in variables C and R, and solve for I.

$$I=2*\sin^{-1}\left(\frac{350[ft]}{2*500[ft]}\right)$$

$$I=40.98^{o}$$

R=500[ft], I=40.98°

$$S=\frac{\pi*R*I}{180^{o}} \leftarrow eq.1$$

Plug in variables R and I into eq.1, then solve for S.

$$S=\frac{\pi*500[ft]*40.98^{o}}{180^{o}}$$

$$S=357.6[ft]$$

S=357.6[ft]

$$S\geq S_{min} \leftarrow ieq.1$$

From ieq.1, the design velocity must correspond to a stopping sight distance at least 357.6 feet.

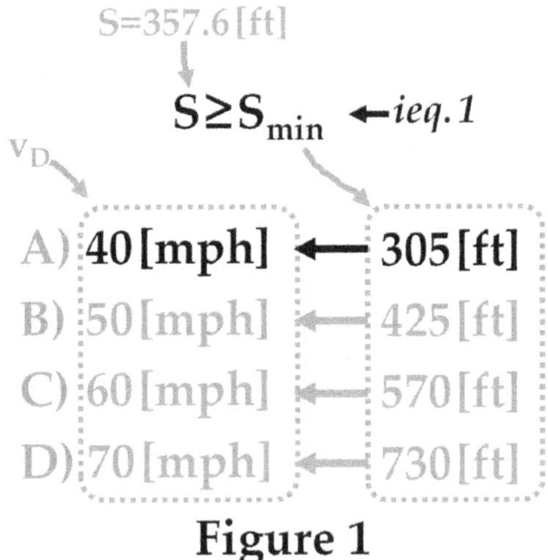

Figure 1

The calculated stopping sight distance, S, is less than the minimum stopping sight distances for design speeds of 50 mph, 60 mph and 70 mph.

Answer: A

Of the four possible solutions, the design speed of 40 miles per hour is the only speed that is safe for this curve.

Solution #26

Find: C_{min} ← the minimum cost of plywood for concrete formwork

Given:

$t \leq 12[weeks]$ ← formwork must be completed in 12 weeks

$A_T=10{,}000[ft^2]$ ← total area of plywood required

$A_{use} \leq 1{,}000[ft^2/week]$ ← maximum weekly plywood use

Plywood Type	Cost per ft^2	Uses
Standard	\$2.25	3
High Density	\$4.00	7

plywood may be reused each week up to either 3 or 7 total uses

A) \$6,000

B) \$6,250

C) \$6,400

D) \$6,650

Analysis:

$$C=QP_S*c_S+QP_{HD}*c_{HD} \quad \leftarrow eq.1$$

quantity of plywood purchased; cost of plywood

Eq.1 computes the cost of plywood.

In eq.1, subscripts "S" and "HD" refer to Standard and High Density, respectively.

Strategy I: Use Only High Density Plywood

Weeks	Type	Qty. Purchased	Cost	Area
1-7	HD	1000[ft^2]	$C_{1\text{-}7}$	$A_{1\text{-}7}$
8-12	HD	$QP_{8\text{-}12}$	$C_{8\text{-}12}$	$A_{8\text{-}12}$

Figure 1

strategy I

$$C_{1\text{-}7,I}=QP_{1\text{-}7,I}*c_{HD} \quad \leftarrow eq.2$$

$QP_{1\text{-}7,I}=1{,}000[ft^2]$ $\quad c_{HD}=\$4/[ft^2]$

Eq.2 computes the cost to purchase 1,000 square feet of high density plywood for the first 7 weeks of formwork, for strategy I.

$$C_{1\text{-}7,I}=1{,}000[ft^2]*\$4/[ft^2]$$

$$C_{1\text{-}7,I}=\$4{,}000$$

Subscript "I" denotes strategy I, and subscript "1-7" denotes weeks 1 through 7.

Solution #26 (cont.)

$$A_{1\text{-}7,I}=QP_{1\text{-}7,I}*t_{1\text{-}7} \leftarrow eq.3$$

$QP_{1\text{-}7,I}=1{,}000\,[ft^2]$ $t_{1\text{-}7}=7$

Eq.3 computes the area of formwork completed using the 1,000 square feet of high density plywood for 7 weeks.

$$A_{1\text{-}7,I}=1{,}000\,[ft^2]*7$$

QP stands for "quantity purchased"

$$A_{1\text{-}7,I}=7{,}000\,[ft^2]$$

Since the total area covered must be 10,000 square feet, eq.4 shows the area covered during weeks 8 through 12 must equal 3,000 square feet.

$$A_{8\text{-}12,I}=A_T-A_{1\text{-}7,I} \leftarrow eq.4$$

$A_T=10{,}000\,[ft^2]$ $A_{1\text{-}7,I}=7{,}000\,[ft^2]$

$$A_{8\text{-}12,I}=10{,}000\,[ft^2]-7{,}000\,[ft^2]$$

$$A_{8\text{-}12,I}=3{,}000\,[ft^2]$$

Eq.5 computes the quantity of high density plywood to purchase for weeks 8 through 12 of formwork.

$$QP_{8\text{-}12,I}=A_{8\text{-}12,I}/t_{8\text{-}12} \leftarrow eq.5$$

$A_{8\text{-}12,I}=3{,}000\,[ft^2]$ $t_{8\text{-}12}=5$

For Strategy I, we'll purchase 600 square feet of high density plywood for formwork on weeks 8 through 12

$$QP_{8\text{-}12,I}=3{,}000\,[ft^2]/5$$

$$QP_{8\text{-}12,I}=600\,[ft^2]$$

Doing so will minimize our the cost for this strategy and still meet the 12 week time requirement.

$$C_{8\text{-}12,I}=QP_{1\text{-}7,I}*c_{HD} \leftarrow eq.6$$

$QP_{8\text{-}12,I}=600\,[ft^2]$ $c_{HD}=\$4/[ft^2]$

Eq.6 computes the cost to purchase 600 square feet of high density plywood.

$$C_{8\text{-}12,I}=600\,[ft^2]*\$4/[ft^2]$$

$$C_{8\text{-}12,I}=\$2{,}400$$

Solution #26 (cont.)

Strategy I: Use Only High Density Plywood

Weeks	Type	Qty. Purchased	Cost	Area
1-7	HD	1000 [ft^2]	\$4,000	7,000 [ft^2]
8-12	HD	600 [ft^2]	\$2,400	3,000 [ft^2]

Figure 2

$$C_I = C_{1\text{-}7,I} + C_{8\text{-}12,I} \quad \leftarrow eq.7$$

$C_{1\text{-}7,I}$=\$4,000 $\quad$ $C_{8\text{-}12,I}$=\$2,400

Eq. 7 computes the total plywood cost associated with strategy I.

$$C_I = \$4{,}000 + \$2{,}400$$

Figure 2 shows the quantity purchased, the cost and the area covered for Strategy I.

$$C_I = \$6{,}400$$

Strategy II: Use a Combination of High Density Plywood and Standard Plywood

Weeks	Type	Qty. Purchased	Cost	Area
1-7	HD	1000 [ft^2]	\$4,000	7,000 [ft^2]
8-10	S	$QP_{8\text{-}10}$	$C_{8\text{-}10}$	$A_{8\text{-}10}$

Figure 3

$$A_{8\text{-}10,II} = A_T - A_{1\text{-}7,II} \quad \leftarrow eq.8$$

A_T=10,000 [ft^2] $\quad$ $A_{1\text{-}7,II}$=7,000 [ft^2]

In Strategy II, we'll complete formwork in 10 weeks because the standard plywood can only be used three times.

$$A_{8\text{-}10,II} = 10{,}000\,[ft^2] - 7{,}000\,[ft^2]$$

Eq. 8 computes the area of formwork left to be completed over weeks 8 through 10.

$$A_{8\text{-}10,II} = 3{,}000\,[ft^2]$$

Solution #26 (cont.)

$$QP_{8\text{-}10,II}=A_{8\text{-}10,II}/t_{8\text{-}12} \leftarrow eq.9$$

$A_{8\text{-}10,II}=3{,}000\,[ft^2]$ $t_{8\text{-}12}=3$

Eq.9 computes the quantity of standard plywood to purchase for formwork on weeks 8 through 10

$$QP_{8\text{-}12,II}=3{,}000\,[ft^2]/3$$

$$QP_{8\text{-}12,II}=1{,}000\,[ft^2]$$

For Strategy II, we'll purchase 1,000 square feet of standard plywood for formwork on weeks 8 through 10.

$$C_{8\text{-}10,II}=QP_{8\text{-}10,II} * c_{HD} \leftarrow eq.10$$

$QP_{8\text{-}12,II}=1{,}000\,[ft^2]$ $c_{HD}=\$2.25/[ft^2]$

Eq.10 computes the cost to purchase 1,000 square feet of standard plywood.

$$C_{8\text{-}12,II}=1{,}000\,[ft^2]*\$2.25/[ft^2]$$

$$C_{8\text{-}12,II}=\$2{,}250$$

Strategy II: Use a Combination of High Density Plywood and Standard Plywood

Weeks	Type	Qty. Purchased	Cost	Area
1-7	HD	1000 [ft²]	$4,000	7,000 [ft²]
8-10	HD	1,000 [ft²]	$2,250	3,000 [ft²]

Figure 3

$$C_{II}=C_{1\text{-}7,II}+C_{8\text{-}10,II} \leftarrow eq.11$$

$C_{1\text{-}7,II}=\$4{,}000$ $C_{8\text{-}10,II}=\$2{,}250$

Eq.11 computes the total plywood cost associated with strategy II.

Strategy II costs less than Strategy I.

$$C_{II}=\$4{,}000+\$2{,}250$$

$$C_{II}=\$6{,}250$$

Answer: **B**

Solution #27

Find: Q_B ← the flow rate through pipe B

Given:

$Q_A=14[gal/min]$ ← the flow rate through pipe A

$d_B=4[in]$ ← the diameter of pipe B

$d_C=6[in]$ ← the diameter of pipe C

$f_B=f_C=0.018$ ← the friction factor through pipes B and C

$L_B=L_C=40[ft]$ ← the length of pipes B and C

pipe schematic: A, B, C, D

A) 3.7[gal/min]
B) 4.4[gal/min]
C) 5.0[gal/min]
D) 5.4[gal/min]

Analysis:

$$Q_B=v_B*A_B \quad \leftarrow eq.1$$

(Q_B: flo rate; v_B: flow velocity; A_B: area)

Eq.1 computes the flow rate in pipe B.

$$A_B=\frac{\pi*d_B^2}{4} \quad \leftarrow eq.2$$

(d_B: diameter of pipe B)

Eq.2 computes the cross-sectional area of pipe B.

$$d_B=4[in]*\frac{1}{12}\left[\frac{ft}{in}\right]=0.333[ft]$$

Convert the diameter of pipe B to feet.

$$A_B=\frac{\pi*d_B^2}{4} \quad \leftarrow eq.2$$

($d_B=0.333[ft]$)

Plug in variable d_B into eq.2, then solve A_B.

$$A_B=\frac{\pi*(0.333[ft])^2}{4}$$

$$A_B=0.08709[ft^2]$$

Solution #27 (cont.)

$$Q_A = Q_B + Q_C \leftarrow eq.3$$

$Q_B = v_B * A_B$ $\quad$ $Q_C = v_C * A_C$

Eq.3 shows the flow rate into a node equals the flow rate out of a node. (Conservation of mass)

Substitute in the velocity times the area for the flow rate in eq.3 for pipe B and pipe C.

$$Q_A = v_B * A_B + v_C * A_C \leftarrow eq.4$$

$$v_B = \frac{Q_A - v_C * A_C}{A_B} \leftarrow eq.5$$

Solve eq.4 for v_B.

diameter of pipe C

$$A_C = \frac{\pi * d_C^2}{4} \leftarrow eq.6$$

Eq.6 computes the cross-sectional area of pipe C.

$$d_C = 6[in] * \frac{1}{12}\left[\frac{ft}{in}\right] = 0.50[ft]$$

Convert the diameter of pipe B to feet.

$d_C = 0.50[ft]$

$$A_C = \frac{\pi * d_C^2}{4} \leftarrow eq.7$$

Plug in variable d_C into eq.7, then solve for A_C.

$$A_C = \frac{\pi * (0.50[ft])^2}{4}$$

$$A_C = 0.1963[ft^2]$$

Eq. 8 shows the headloss through pipe B equals the headloss through pipe C. (Conservation of energy)

$$h_{L,B} = h_{L,C} \leftarrow eq.8$$

Write out the headloss terms in eq.8 using the Darcy's headloss equation.

friction factor, pipe length, velocity

$$\frac{f_B * L_B * v_B^2}{2 * D_{e,B} * g} = \frac{f_C * L_C * v_C^2}{2 * D_{e,C} * g} \leftarrow eq.9$$

effective diameter, gravitational acceleration

The friction factor, length and constant terms all cancel out of eq.9 because they are equal for pipes B and C.

Solution #27 (cont.)

The effective diameter of a circular pipe is the pipe diameter.

$$\frac{v_B^2}{D_{e,B}} = \frac{v_C^2}{D_{e,C}} \leftarrow eq.10$$

$D_{e,B}=d_B$ $D_{e,C}=d_C$

In eq.10, substitute in d for D_e, then solve for v_C.

$$\frac{v_B^2}{d_B} = \frac{v_C^2}{d_C}$$

$d_C=6$ [in]

$$v_C=\sqrt{\frac{v_B^{2} * d_C}{d_B}} \leftarrow eq.11$$

$d_B=4$ [in]

Plug in variables d_B and d_C into eq.11, then simplify.

$$v_C=\sqrt{\frac{v_B^{2} * 6[in]}{4[in]}}$$

$$v_C=1.225 * v_B$$

$$Q_A=14\left[\frac{gal}{min}\right] * \frac{1}{7.48}\left[\frac{ft^3}{gal}\right] * \frac{1}{60}\left[\frac{min}{s}\right] \leftarrow eq.12$$

Eq.12 converts the flow rate to units of cubic feet per second.

$$Q_A=0.0312[ft^3/s]$$

$Q_A=0.0312$ [ft³/s] $v_C=1.225 * v_B$

$$v_B=\frac{Q_A - v_C * A_C}{A_B} \leftarrow eq.5$$

$A_B=0.08709$ [ft²] $A_C=0.1963$ [ft²]

Plug in variables Q_A, V_C, A_B and A_C into eq.5, then solve for v_B.

$$v_B=\frac{0.0312[ft^3/s] - 1.225 * v_B * 0.1963[ft^2]}{0.08709[ft^2]}$$

$$v_B=0.0952[ft/s]$$

Solution #27 (cont.)

$A_B = 0.08709\,[ft^2]$

$$Q_B = v_B * A_B \quad \leftarrow eq.1$$

$v_B = 0.0952\,[ft/s]$

Plug in variables v_B and A_B, into eq.1, then solve for Q_B.

$$Q_B = 0.0952\,[ft/s] * 0.08709\,[ft^2]$$

$$Q_B = 8.29 * 10^{-3}\left[\frac{ft^3}{s}\right] * 60\left[\frac{s}{min}\right] * 7.48\left[\frac{gal}{ft^3}\right]$$

Converts the units to gallons per minute

$$Q_B = 3.72\,[gal/min]$$

<u>Answer</u>: **A**

Solution #28

Find: K ← hydraulic conductivity of the sand

Given:

$Q=6.13\,[ft^3/day]$ ← flow rate

$h_1=15\,[in]$ ← upstream head

$h_2=6\,[in]$ ← downstream head

$L=5\,[in]$ ← length of sand sample

$V_V=18.86\,[in^3]$

$V_T=62.58\,[in^3]$

} volume of voids and total volume of the sand

$A_g=12.57\,[in^2]$ ← gross area of the permeameter

A) 120 [ft/day]

B) 130 [ft/day]

C) 140 [ft/day]

D) 150 [ft/day]

Analysis:

$$Q=K*i*A_g*\eta \quad \leftarrow eq.1$$

(Q: flow rate; K: hydraulic conductivity; i: gradient; A_g: gross area; η: porosity)

Eq.1 computes the flow rate of a fluid through a porous media.

$$K=\frac{Q}{i*A_g*\eta} \quad \leftarrow eq.2$$

Solve eq.1 for the hydraulic conductivity, K.

$$i=\frac{h_1-h_2}{L} \quad \leftarrow eq.3$$

($h_1=15\,[in]$, $h_2=6\,[in]$, $L=5\,[in]$)

Eq.3 computes the gradient across the sand sample by dividing the head loss across the sand sample by the length of the sample.

$$i=\frac{15\,[in]-6\,[in]}{5\,[in]}$$

Plug in variables h_1, h_2 and L into eq.3, then solve for i.

$$i=1.8$$

$$A_g=12.57\,[in^2]*\left(\frac{1}{12}\left[\frac{ft}{in}\right]\right)^2 \quad \leftarrow eq.4$$

Eq.4 converts the gross area from square inches to square feet.

Solution #28 (cont.)

$$A_g=0.0873\,[ft^2]$$

$V_V=18.86\,[in^3]$

$$\eta=\frac{V_V}{V_T} \leftarrow eq.5$$

$V_T=62.58\,[in^3]$

Eq.5 computes the porosity of the sand by diving the volume of voids by the total volume.

Plug in variables V_V and V_T into eq.5, then solve for η.

$$\eta=\frac{18.86\,[in^3]}{62.58\,[in^3]}$$

$$\eta=0.30$$

$Q=6.13\,[ft^3/day]$

$$K=\frac{Q}{i*A_g*\eta} \leftarrow eq.2$$

$i=1.8$ $\quad$ $A_g=0.0873\,[ft^2]$ $\quad$ $\eta=0.30$

Plug in variables Q, i, A_g and η into eq.2, then solve for K.

$$K=\frac{6.13\,[ft^3/day]}{1.8*0.0873\,[ft^2]*0.30}$$

$$K=130.0\,[ft/day]$$

Answer: B

Solution #29

the minimum number of engineers to be added to the team so that engineering is no longer the bottleneck task.

Find: ΔN_E

Given:

predecessor task of task i; the number of people working on task i, [workers]; production rate of task i, [acres/(hour*workers)]

i	$Task_i$	$Pred_i$	N_i	U_i
S	Surveying	-	8	0.10
E	Engineering	S	4	0.12
G	Grading	E	26	0.04

A) 2
B) 3
C) 4
D) 5

Analysis:

Figure 1

Figure 1 shows the order of tasks, based on the predecessors identified in the given table.

The "bottleneck" task is the task which produces at the slowest rate.

$$P_i = N_i * U_i \leftarrow eq.1$$

production rate; number of workers; production rate per worker

Eq. 1 computes the production rate of task i.

$$(N_E + \Delta N_E) * U_E > \min(P_S, P_G) \leftarrow ieq.1$$

additional number of engineers; production rate of surveyors and graders; initial number of engineers; production rate per engineer

Replace subscript i with S, E, or G to represent surveying, engineering or grading.

Ieq. 2 identifies the number of additional engineers, ΔN_E.

$$\Delta N_E > \frac{\min(P_S, P_G)}{U_E} - N_E \leftarrow ieq.2$$

Ieq. 2 isolates the ΔN_E term from ieq. 1.

$N_S = 8$ [surveyors] $U_S = 0.10$ [acre/(hr*surveyor)]

$$P_S = N_S * U_S \leftarrow eq.2$$

Eq. 2 computes the production rate of the surveying team.

Solution #29 (cont.)

Plug in variables N_S and U_S into eq.2, then solve for P_S.

$$P_S=8[\text{surveyors}]*0.10[\text{acre}/(\text{hr}*\text{surveyor})]$$

$$P_S=0.80[\text{acre}/\text{hr}]$$

Eq.3 calculates the production rate of the grading team.

$N_G=26[\text{graders}]$ $U_G=0.04[\text{acre}/(\text{hr}*\text{grader})]$

$$P_G=N_G*U_G \quad \leftarrow eq.3$$

Plug in variables N_G and U_G into eq.3, then solve for P_G.

$$P_G=26[\text{graders}]*0.04[\text{acre}/(\text{hr}*\text{grader})]$$

$$P_G=1.04[\text{acre}/\text{hr}]$$

$P_S=0.80[\text{acre}/\text{hr}]$ $P_G=1.04[\text{acre}/\text{hr}]$

$$\Delta N_E>\frac{\min(P_S,P_G)}{U_E}-N_E \quad \leftarrow ieq.2$$

$N_E=4[\text{engineers}]$

$U_E=0.12[\text{acre}/(\text{hr}*\text{engineer})]$

Plug in P_S, P_G, U_E and N_E into ieq.2, then solve for ΔN_E.

$$\Delta N_E>\frac{\min(0.80[\text{acre}/\text{hr}],1.04[\text{acre}/\text{hr}])}{0.12[\text{acre}/(\text{hr}*\text{engineer})]}-4[\text{engineers}]$$

$$\Delta N_E>2.66[\text{engineers}]$$

Round 2.66 up to 3.

$$\Delta N_E=3[\text{engineers}]$$

After 3 engineers are added to the team, the engineering task is no longer the bottleneck task.

Answer: **B**

Solution #30

Find: $Q_{30\text{-}40}$ ← the flow rate between minute 30 and minute 40

Given:

$V_T=3.321*10^5[gal]$
↑ total volume of runoff from minute 0 to minute 60

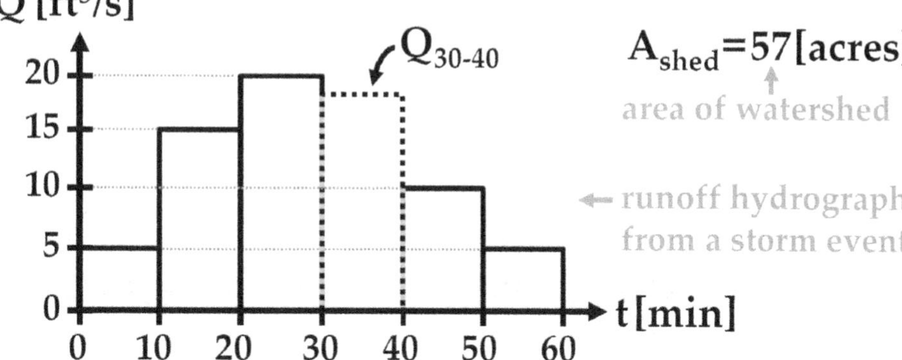

$A_{shed}=57[acres]$
↑ area of watershed

← runoff hydrograph from a storm event

A) 16[ft³/s]
B) 17[ft³/s]
C) 18[ft³/s]
D) 19[ft³/s]

Analysis:

$$V_T=\Sigma V_i=\Delta t*\Sigma Q_i \quad \leftarrow eq.1$$

total volume (V_T), duration of period (Δt), flow rate of period i (Q_i)

Eq.1 computes the total volume of runoff from the storm event.

Expand the summation term in eq 1.

$$V_T=\Delta t*(Q_{0\text{-}10}+Q_{10\text{-}20}+Q_{20\text{-}30}+Q_{30\text{-}40}+Q_{40\text{-}50}+Q_{50\text{-}60}) \quad \leftarrow eq.2$$

Solve eq.2 for $Q_{30\text{-}40}$.

$$Q_{30\text{-}40}=\frac{V_T}{\Delta t}-Q_{0\text{-}10}-Q_{10\text{-}20}-Q_{20\text{-}30}-Q_{40\text{-}50}-Q_{50\text{-}60} \quad \leftarrow eq.3$$

$$V_T=3.321*10^5[gal]*\frac{1}{7.48}\left[\frac{ft^3}{gal}\right] \quad \leftarrow eq.4$$

Eq.4 converts the total volume to cubic feet.

$$V_T=4.440*10^4[ft^3]$$

$$\Delta t=10[min]*60\left[\frac{s}{min}\right] \quad \leftarrow eq.5$$

Eq.5 converts the duration of each 10-minute period to seconds.

$$\Delta t=600[s]$$

Solution #30 (cont.)

Plug in variables V_T, d_T, and all known Q values into eq.3, then solve for $Q_{30\text{-}40}$.

$V_T=4.440*10^4\,[ft^3]$ $\quad Q_{10\text{-}20}=15\,[ft^3/s]$ $\quad Q_{40\text{-}50}=10\,[ft^3/s]$

$$Q_{30\text{-}40}=\frac{V_T}{\Delta t}-Q_{0\text{-}10}-Q_{10\text{-}20}-Q_{20\text{-}30}-Q_{40\text{-}50}-Q_{50\text{-}60} \leftarrow eq.3$$

$\Delta t=600\,[s]$ $\quad Q_{0\text{-}10}=5\,[ft^3/s]$ $\quad Q_{20\text{-}30}=20\,[ft^3/s]$ $\quad Q_{50\text{-}60}=5\,[ft^3/s]$

$$Q_{30\text{-}40}=\frac{4.440*10^4[ft^3]}{600[s]}-5[ft^3/s]-15[ft^3/s]-20[ft^3/s]-10[ft^3/s]-5[ft^3/s]$$

$$Q_{30\text{-}40}=19[ft^3/s]$$

Answer: D

Solution #31

Find: τ @ σ=3,000[lb/ft^2] ← the shear stress of the soil in a direct shear test when 3,000 pounds per foot of normal stress is applied

Given:

σ_1=180[lb/in^2]

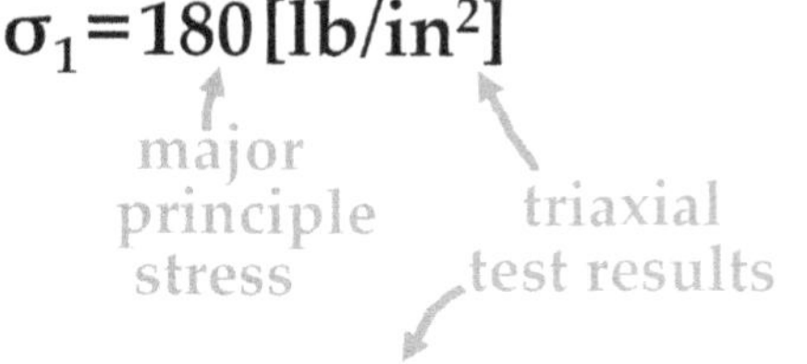

σ_3=60[lb/in^2]

minor principle stress

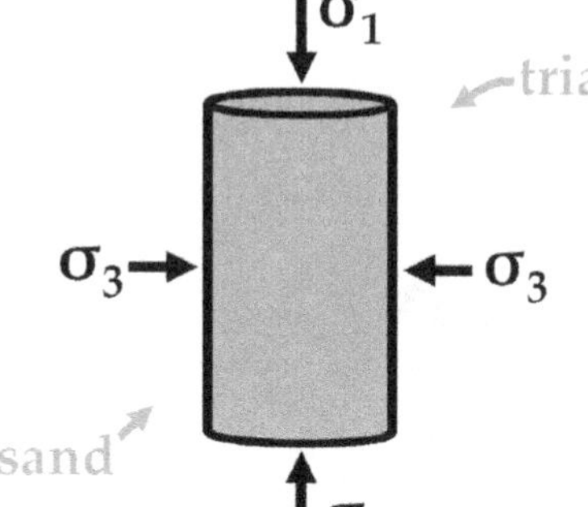

A) 1,500[lb/ft^2]

B) 1,730[lb/ft^2]

C) 2,620[lb/ft^2]

D) 5,200[lb/ft^2]

Analysis:

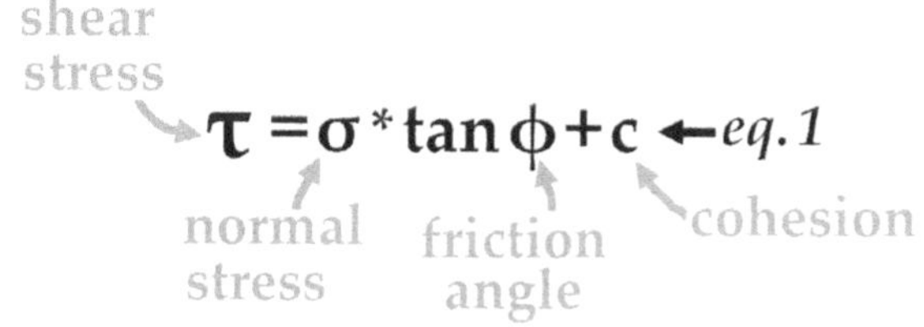

$$\tau = \sigma * \tan\phi + c \quad \leftarrow eq.1$$

Eq.1 computes the shear stress in the soil.

$$\sigma=3{,}000\,[\text{lb/ft}^2]$$

From the problem statement we know the normal stress is 3,000 pounds per foot squared.

$$c=0\,[\text{lb/ft}^2]$$

Since sand is assumed to be cohesionless, we set c equal to zero.

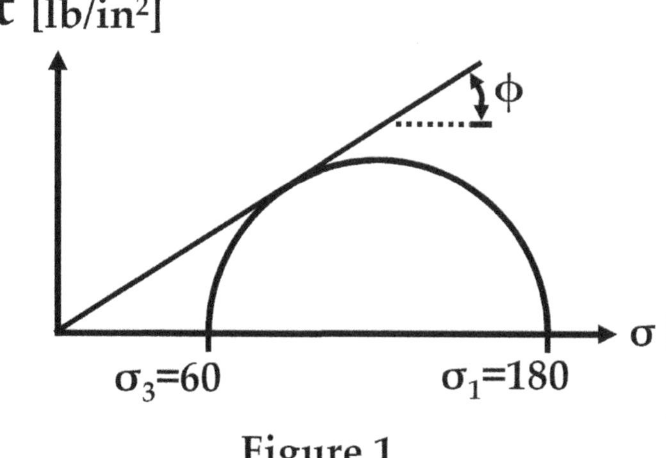

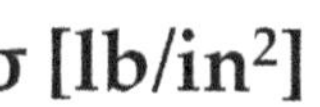

Figure 1

Figure 1 shows the major and minor principle stress plotted, and Mohr's circle sketched out.

The friction angle equals the slope of the failure envelope.

The failure envelope passes through the origin because sand is assumed to be cohesionless.

Solution #31 (cont.)

Figure 2 identifies a right triangle, where C is the average principle stress and R is the maximum shear stress.

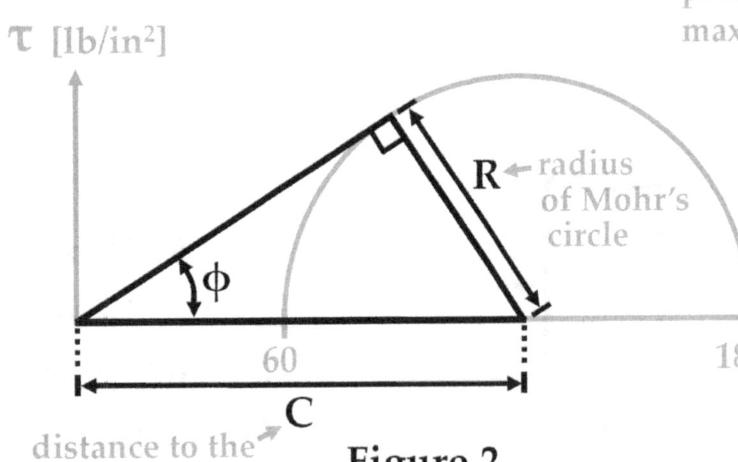

Figure 2

From Figure 2, we can use trigonometry to derive an equation for the friction angle.

$$\sin\phi = R/C \leftarrow eq.2$$

(R: maximum shear stress; C: average principle stress)

Eq.2 computes the sin of the friction angle. Solve eq.2 for phi.

$$\phi = \sin^{-1}(R/C) \leftarrow eq.3$$

$\sigma_1 = 180\,[lb/in^2]$ $\sigma_3 = 60\,[lb/in^2]$

$$R = \frac{\sigma_1 - \sigma_3}{2} \leftarrow eq.4$$

Eq.4 computes the maximum shear stress, R.

$$R = \frac{180[lb/in^2] - 60[lb/in^2]}{2}$$

Plug in σ_1 and σ_3 into eq.4, then solve for R.

$$R = 60\,[lb/in^2]$$

$\sigma_1 = 180\,[lb/in^2]$ $\sigma_3 = 60\,[lb/in^2]$

$$C = \frac{\sigma_1 + \sigma_3}{2} \leftarrow eq.5$$

Eq.5 computes the average principle stress in the soil, C.

Plug in σ_1 and σ_3 into eq.5, then solve for C.

Solution #31 (cont.)

$$C=\frac{180[lb/in^2]+60[lb/in^2]}{2}$$

$$C=120[lb/in^2]$$

R=60 [lb/in²] C=120 [lb/in²]

$$\phi=\sin^{-1}(R/C) \leftarrow eq.3$$

Plug in variables R and C into eq.3, then solve for ϕ.

$$\phi=\sin^{-1}(60[lb/in^2]/120[lb/in^2])$$

$$\phi=30^\circ$$

$\phi=30^\circ$ c=0 [lb/ft²]

$$\tau=\sigma*\tan\phi+c \leftarrow eq.1$$

$\sigma=3{,}000\,[lb/ft^2]$

Plug in variables σ, ϕ and c into eq.1, then solve for τ.

$$\tau=3{,}000[lb/ft^2]*\tan(30^\circ)+0[lb/ft^2]$$

$$\tau=1{,}732[lb/ft^2]$$

Answer: **B**

Solution #32

Find: v_i ← the initial velocity of the car

Given:

$S=45.5\,[m]$ ← stopping sight distance

$t_p=2.5\,[s]$ ← perception-reaction time

$a=3.1\,[m/s^2]$ ← acceleration (the car slowing down to a stop)

$G=4\%$ (uphill) ← grade

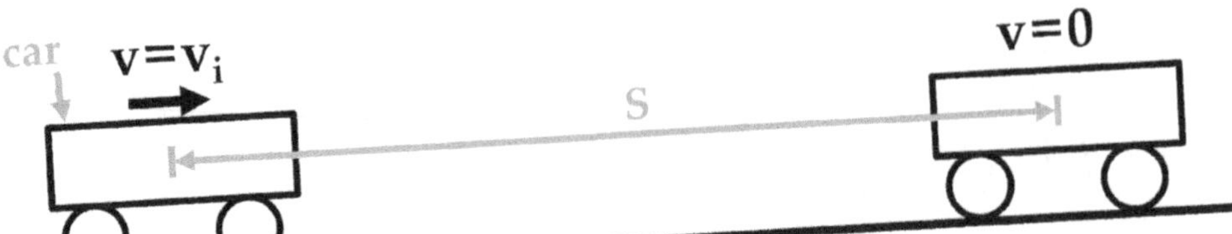

A) 40 [km/hr]

B) 50 [km/hr]

C) 60 [km/hr]

D) 70 [km/hr]

Analysis:

$$S=0.278\left[\frac{m*hr}{km*s}\right]*t_p*v_{i,km/hr}+\frac{v_{i,km/hr}^2}{254*(f+G)} \leftarrow eq.1$$

(S: stopping sight distance; t_p: perception-reaction time; $v_{i,km/hr}$: initial velocity of the car; f: coefficient of friction; G: grade (decimal))

Eq.1 computes the stopping distance, S, as a function of the velocity.

Eq.1 is a quadratic equation. Solve eq. 1 for the initial velocity, v_i.

$$v_{i,km/hr}=\frac{-0.278\left[\frac{m*hr}{km*s}\right]*t_p\pm\sqrt{\left(0.278\left[\frac{m*hr}{km*s}\right]*t_p\right)^2-4*\left(\frac{3.937*10^{-3}}{f+G}\right)*(-S)}}{2*\left(\frac{3.937*10^{-3}}{f+G}\right)} \leftarrow eq.2$$

$$G=4\%=0.04 \leftarrow eq.3$$

Eq.3 identifies the grade of the road, as a decimal value.

$$f=\frac{a}{g}=\frac{3.1[m/s^2]}{9.81[m/s^2]}=0.316 \leftarrow eq.4$$

($a=3.1\,[m/s^2]$; $g=9.81\,[m/s^2]$)

Eq.4 computes the friction coefficient. Plug in variables a and g, then solve for f.

Solution #32 (cont.)

We'll drop the units from eq. 2 and remember S is in meters, t_p is in seconds, and v is in kilometers per hour.

$t_p=2.5\,[s]$, $S=45.5\,[m]$, $f=0.316$, $G=0.04$

$$v_i=\frac{-0.278*t_p \pm \sqrt{(0.278*t_p)^2 - 4*\left(\frac{3.937*10^{-3}}{f+G}\right)*(-S)}}{\left(\frac{7.874*10^{-3}}{f+G}\right)} \quad \leftarrow eq.\,2$$

Plug in the known values into eq.2, then solve for the initial velocity, v_i.

$$v_i=\frac{-0.278*2.5 \pm \sqrt{(0.278*2.5)^2 - 4*\left(\frac{3.937*10^{-3}}{0.316+0.04}\right)*(-45.5)}}{\left(\frac{7.874*10^{-3}}{0.316+0.04}\right)}$$

$$v_i=-102.8\,[km/hr],\ 40\,[km/hr]$$

The quadratic formula yielded two solutions. We'll choose the positive solution, which is 40 kilometers per hour.

$$v_i=40\,[km/hr]$$

Answer: A

Solution #33

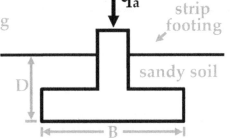

Find: q_a ← the allowable bearing capacity

Given:

$D=1[m]$ ← depth of footing

$B=2[m]$ ← base width of footing

$F=2$ ← safety factor

$\phi=40^o$ ← angle of internal friction

$W=9{,}560[N]$, $V=0.478[m^3]$ } weight and volume of a sample of the soil

use Terzaghi bearing capacity factors

groundwater not present

strip footing

sandy soil

A) $1.63*10^6[N/m^2]$

B) $1.82*10^6[N/m^2]$

C) $2.01*10^6[N/m^2]$

D) $3.63*10^6[N/m^2]$

Analysis:

$$q_a=\frac{q_{net}}{F} \leftarrow eq.1$$

allowable bearing capacity; net bearing capacity; safety factor

Eq.1 calculates the allowable bearing capacity for a strip footing.

$$q_{net}=0.5*\gamma*B*N_\gamma+c*N_c+\gamma*D*N_q \leftarrow eq.2$$

footing width; bearing capacity factors; unit weight of the soil; cohesion c=0; footing depth

Eq.2 calculates the net bearing capacity of the footing.

$$q_{net}=0.5*\gamma*B*N_\gamma+\gamma*D*N_q \leftarrow eq.3$$

Sandy soils are assumed to be cohesionless. Plug in zero for c in eq.2, then simplify.

$$\text{for } \phi=40^o \rightarrow \begin{cases} N_q=81.3 \\ N_\gamma=100.4 \end{cases}$$

Bearing capacity factors are based on the angle of internal friction and can be looked up in a table.

The problem specifies we use Terzaghi bearing capacity factors.

$$\gamma=\frac{W}{V} \leftarrow eq.4$$

($W=9{,}560[N]$, $V=0.478[m^3]$)

Eq.4 computes the total unit weight of the soil. Plug in variables W and V, then solve for γ.

Solution #33 (cont.)

$$\gamma = \frac{9{,}560\,[N]}{0.478\,[m^3]}$$

$$\gamma = 20{,}000\,[N/m^3]$$

Plug in variables γ, D, B, N_γ and N_q into eq.3, then solve for q_{net}.

$\gamma=20{,}000\,[N/m^3]$ D=1 [m]

$$q_{net} = 0.5 * \gamma * B * N_\gamma + \gamma * D * N_q \leftarrow eq.3$$

B=2 [m] $N_\gamma=100.4$ $N_q=81.3$

$$q_{net} = 0.5 * 20{,}000\,[N/m^3] * 2\,[m] * 100.4 + 20{,}000[N/m^3] * 1[m] * 81.3$$

$$q_{net} = 3.634*10^6\,[N/m^2]$$

Plug in variables q_{net} and F into eq.1, then solve for the allowable bearing capacity, q_a.

$q_{net}=3.634*10^6\,[N/m^3]$

$$q_a = \frac{q_{net}}{F} \leftarrow eq.1$$

F=2

$$q_a = \frac{3.634*10^6\,[N/m^2]}{2}$$

$$q_a = 1.817*10^6\,[N/m^2]$$

Answer: B

Find: σ_1 ← the larger principle normal stress

Given:

σ_y=-10,500[lb/in^2]
↑ normal stress in the y-direction (compression)

σ_x=3,400[lb/in^2]
↑ normal stress in the x-direction (tension)

$\tau_{xy,max}$=9,050[lb/in^2]
↑ the maximum shear stress

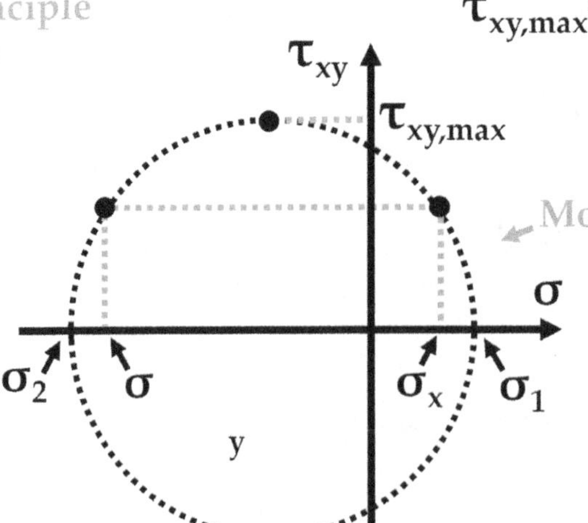

Mohr's circle

A) 5,500[lb/in^2]
B) 5,800[lb/in^2]
C) 8,830[lb/in^2]
D) 9,050[lb/in^2]

Analysis:

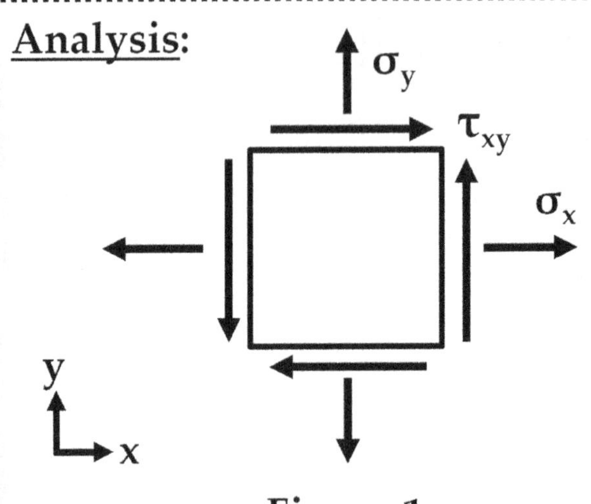

Figure 1

Figure 1 shows a free body diagram of the element, where both normal stresses are shown in tension.

In the y-direction the stress is compressive (a negative value). In the x-direction the stress is tensile (a positive value).

Eq.1 computes the larger principle normal stress.

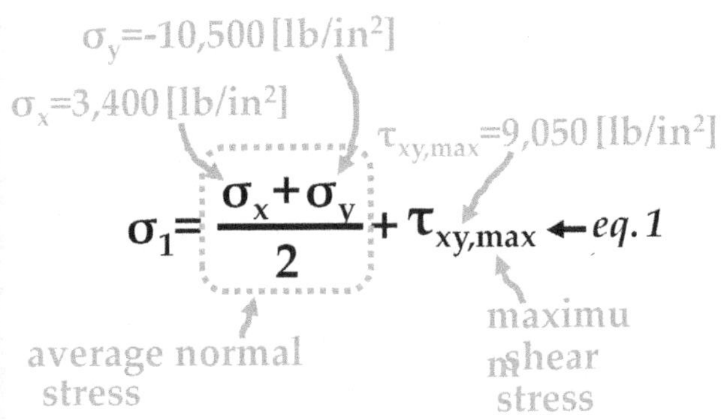

In eq.1, the first term equals the average normal stress, or the "center of Mohr's circle" and the second term equals the maximum shear stress, or the "radius of Mohr's circle."

Plug in variables σ_x $\sigma_{y,}$ and $\tau_{xy,max}$ into eq.1, then solve for σ_1.

$$\sigma_1=\frac{3{,}400[lb/in^2]+(-10{,}500[lb/in^2])}{2}+9{,}050[lb/in^2]$$

σ_1=5,500[lb/in^2]

Answer: A

Solution #35

Find: V_{nc} ← the net volume of cut material

Given: cut and fill data

STA	Cut Area	Fill Area
0+00	0 [ft²]	0 [ft²]
0+25	62 [ft²]	21 [ft²]
0+50	80 [ft²]	34 [ft²]
0+75	45 [ft²]	24 [ft²]
1+00	0 [ft²]	0 [ft²]

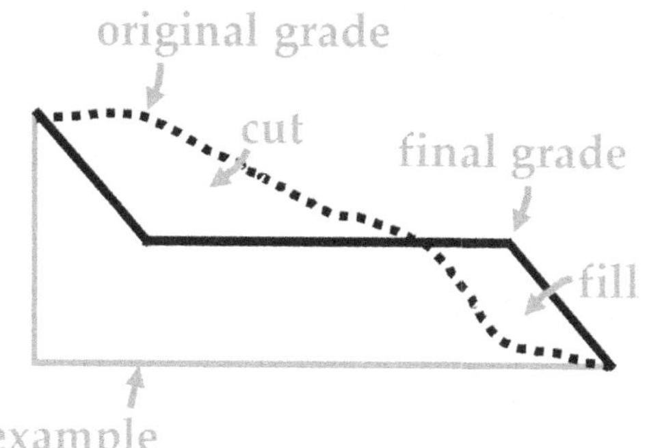

A) 100 [yd³]
B) 250 [yd³]
C) 2,000 [yd³]
D) 2,700 [yd³]

Analysis:

net volume of cut material

$$V_{nc} = \Sigma V_c - \Sigma V_f \quad \leftarrow eq. 1$$

total volume of cut material; total volume of fill material

Eq. 1 computes the net volume of cut material.

Eq. 2 computes the total volume of cut material.

$$\Sigma V_c = V_{c,0+00\text{-}0+25} + V_{c,0+25\text{-}0+50} + V_{c,0+50\text{-}0+75} + V_{c,0+75\text{-}1+00} \quad \leftarrow eq. 2$$

volume of cut material between specified stations

Eq. 3 computes the volume of cut material between station 0+00 and station 0+25.

$A_{c,0+00} = 0\,[ft^2]$ $A_{c,0+25} = 62\,[ft^2]$

$$V_{c,0+00\text{-}0+25} = \left(\frac{A_{c,0+00} + A_{c,0+25}}{2}\right) * (STA_{0+25} - STA_{0+00}) \quad \leftarrow eq. 3$$

$STA_{0+25} - STA_{0+00} = 25\,[ft]$

$$V_{c,0+00\text{-}0+25} = \left(\frac{0\,[ft^2] + 62\,[ft^2]}{2}\right) * 25\,[ft]$$

$$V_{c,0+00\text{-}0+25} = 775\,[ft^3]$$

In eq. 3, $A_{C,0+00}$ and $A_{C,0+25}$ represent the area cut at stations 0+00 and 0+25, respectively.

Solution #35 (cont.)

Eq.4 computes the volume of cut material between station 0+25 and station 0+50.

$A_{c,0+25}=62\,[ft^2]$ $A_{c,0+50}=80\,[ft^2]$

$$V_{c,0+25\text{-}0+50}=\left(\frac{A_{c,0+25}+A_{c,0+50}}{2}\right)*(STA_{0+50}-STA_{0+25}) \quad \leftarrow eq.4$$

$STA_{0+50}-STA_{0+25}=25\,[ft]$

$$V_{c,0+25\text{-}0+50}=\left(\frac{62\,[ft^2]+80\,[ft^2]}{2}\right)*25\,[ft]$$

$$V_{c,0+25\text{-}0+50}=1{,}775\,[ft^3]$$

Eq.5 computes the volume of cut material between station 0+50 and station 0+75.

$A_{c,0+50}=80\,[ft^2]$ $A_{c,0+75}=45\,[ft^2]$

$$V_{c,0+50\text{-}0+75}=\left(\frac{A_{c,0+50}+A_{c,0+75}}{2}\right)*(STA_{0+75}-STA_{0+50}) \quad \leftarrow eq.5$$

$STA_{0+75}-STA_{0+50}=25\,[ft]$

$$V_{c,0+50\text{-}0+75}=\left(\frac{80\,[ft^2]+45\,[ft^2]}{2}\right)*25\,[ft]$$

$$V_{c,0+50\text{-}0+75}=1{,}563\,[ft^3]$$

Volumes are rounded to the nearest cubic foot.

Eq.6 computes the volume of cut material between station 0+75 and station 1+00.

$A_{c,0+75}=45\,[ft^2]$ $A_{c,1+00}=0\,[ft^2]$

$$V_{c,0+75\text{-}1+00}=\left(\frac{A_{c,0+75}+A_{c,1+00}}{2}\right)*(STA_{1+00}-STA_{0+75}) \quad \leftarrow eq.6$$

$STA_{1+00}-STA_{0+75}=25\,[ft]$

$$V_{c,0+75\text{-}1+00}=\left(\frac{45\,[ft^2]+0\,[ft^2]}{2}\right)*25\,[ft]$$

$$V_{c,0+75\text{-}1+00}=563\,[ft^3]$$

Solution #35 (cont.)

Plug in the known volumes into the right hand side of eq.2, then solve for ΣV_c.

$V_{c,0+00-0+25}=775\,[ft^3]$ $V_{c,0+50-0+75}=1{,}563\,[ft^3]$

$$\Sigma V_c = V_{c,0+00-0+25} + V_{c,0+25-0+50} + V_{c,0+50-0+75} + V_{c,0+75-1+00} \leftarrow eq.2$$

$V_{c,0+25-0+50}=1{,}775\,[ft^3]$ $V_{c,0+75-1+00}=563\,[ft^3]$

$$\Sigma V_c = 775\,[ft^3] + 1{,}775\,[ft^3] + 1{,}563\,[ft^3] + 563\,[ft^3]$$

$$\Sigma V_c = 4{,}676\,[ft^3]$$

Eq.7 computes the total volume of fill material.

$$\Sigma V_f = V_{f,0+00-0+25} + V_{f,0+25-0+50} + V_{f,0+50-0+75} + V_{f,0+75-1+00} \leftarrow eq.7$$

volume of fill material between specified stations

Eq.8 computes the volume of fill material between station 0+00 and station 0+25.

$A_{f,0+00}=0\,[ft^2]$ $A_{f,0+25}=21\,[ft^2]$

$$V_{f,0+00-0+25} = \left(\frac{A_{f,0+00} + A_{f,0+25}}{2}\right) * (STA_{0+25} - STA_{0+00}) \leftarrow eq.8$$

$STA_{0+25} - STA_{0+00} = 25\,[ft]$

$$V_{f,0+00-0+25} = \left(\frac{0\,[ft^2] + 21\,[ft^2]}{2}\right) * 25\,[ft]$$

$$V_{f,0+00-0+25} = 263\,[ft^3]$$

Eq.9 computes the volume of fill material between station 0+25 and station 0+50.

$A_{f,0+25}=21\,[ft^2]$ $A_{f,0+50}=34\,[ft^2]$

$$V_{f,0+25-0+50} = \left(\frac{A_{f,0+25} + A_{f,0+50}}{2}\right) * (STA_{0+50} - STA_{0+25}) \leftarrow eq.9$$

$STA_{0+50} - STA_{0+25} = 25\,[ft]$

Solution #35 (cont.)

$$V_{f,0+25-0+50}=\left(\frac{21[ft^2]+34[ft^2]}{2}\right)*25[ft]$$

$$V_{f,0+25-0+50}=688[ft^3]$$

Eq. 10 computes the volume of fill material between station 0+50 and station 0+75.

$A_{f,0+50}=34[ft^2]$ $A_{f,0+75}=24[ft^2]$

$$V_{f,0+50-0+75}=\left(\frac{A_{f,0+50}+A_{f,0+75}}{2}\right)*(STA_{0+75}-STA_{0+50}) \leftarrow eq.10$$

$STA_{0+75}-STA_{0+50}=25[ft]$

$$V_{f,0+50-0+75}=\left(\frac{34[ft^2]+24[ft^2]}{2}\right)*25[ft]$$

$$V_{f,0+25-0+50}=725[ft^3]$$

Eq. 11 computes the volume of fill material between station 1+00 and station 0+75.

$A_{f,0+75}=24[ft^2]$ $A_{f,1+00}=0[ft^2]$

$$V_{f,0+75-1+00}=\left(\frac{A_{f,0+75}+A_{f,1+00}}{2}\right)*(STA_{1+00}-STA_{0+75}) \leftarrow eq.11$$

$STA_{1+00}-STA_{0+75}=25[ft]$

$$V_{f,0+75-1+00}=\left(\frac{24[ft^2]+0[ft^2]}{2}\right)*25[ft]$$

$$V_{f,0+75-1+00}=300[ft^3]$$

Plug in the known volumes into the right hand side of eq. 7, then solve for ΣV_f.

$V_{f,0+25-0+50}=688[ft^3]$

$$\Sigma V_f=V_{f,0+00-0+25}+V_{f,0+25-0+50}+V_{f,0+50-0+75}+V_{f,0+75-1+00} \leftarrow eq.7$$

$V_{f,0+00-0+25}=263[ft^3]$ $V_{f,0+50-0+75}=725[ft^3]$ $V_{f,0+75-1+00}=300[ft^3]$

Solution #35 (cont.)

$$\Sigma V_f = 263[ft^3] + 688[ft^3] + 725[ft^3] + 300[ft^3]$$

$$\Sigma V_f = 1,976[ft^3]$$

$$V_{nc} = \Sigma V_c - \Sigma V_f \leftarrow eq.1$$

$\Sigma V_c = 4,676[ft^3]$ $\Sigma V_f = 1,976[ft^3]$

Plug in variables ΣV_c and ΣV_f into eq. 1, then solve for V_{nc}.

$$V_{nc} = 4,676[ft^3] - 1,976[ft^3]$$

$$V_{nc} = 2,700[ft^3] * \frac{1}{27}\left[\frac{yd^3}{ft^3}\right]$$

Convert the net volume of cut material to units of cubic yards.

$$V_{nc} = 100[yd^3]$$

Answer: A

Solution #36

Find: t ← the time required to completely fill the conical tank with water.

Given:

$P=2.5[hp]$ ← power of the pump

$d_T=50[ft]$ ← tank diameter (at the top)

$h_T=50[ft]$ ← tank height

$\eta_p=80\%$ ← pump efficiency

$\Delta h=200[ft]$ ← total head lift seen by the pump

assume the tank starts empty

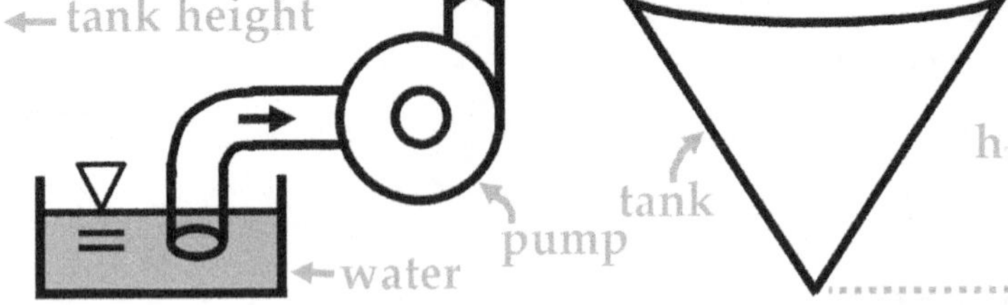

A) 1.3[days]
B) 3.4[days]
C) 4.3[days]
D) 12.9[days]

Analysis:

$$t=\frac{V_T}{Q} \leftarrow eq.1$$

(V_T = volume of tank, Q = flow rate)

Eq. 1 computes the time required to fill the tank.

$$V_T=\frac{\pi*d_T^2*h_T}{12} \leftarrow eq.2$$

($d_T=50[ft]$, $h_T=50[ft]$)

Eq. 2 computes the volume of a cone. Plug in variables d_T and h_T into eq. 2, then solve for V_T.

$$V_T=\frac{\pi*(50[ft])^2*50[ft]}{12}$$

$$V_T=3.272*10^4[ft^3]*7.48\left[\frac{gal}{ft^3}\right] \leftarrow eq.3$$

Eq. 3 converts the volume of the tank to gallons.

$$V_T=2.448*10^5[gal]$$

$$P=\frac{\Delta h*Q*SG}{3{,}956*\eta_P} \leftarrow eq.4$$

(P = pump power [hp], Δh = change in head [ft], Q = flow rate [gal/min], SG = specific gravity, η_P = pump efficiency)

Eq. 4 computes the power of the pump. The units specified in the equation.

Solution #36 (cont.)

Solve eq.4 for the flow rate, Q.

P=2.5 [hp] η_P=80%=0.80

$$Q=\frac{3,956*P*\eta_P}{\Delta h*SG}$$

Δh=200 [ft] SG=1.00

Plug in variables P, η_P, Δh and SG, then solve for Q.

The specific gravity of water is 1.

$$Q=\frac{3,956*2.5[hp]*0.80}{200[ft]*1.00}$$

Recall the units for flow rate in this equation are in units of gallons per minute.

$$Q=39.56[gal/min]$$

V_T=2.448*10^5 [gal]

$$t=\frac{V_T}{Q} \leftarrow eq.1$$

Q=39.56 [gal/min]

Plug in variables Q and V_T into eq.1, then solve for t.

$$t=\frac{2.448*10^5[gal]}{39.56[gal/min]}$$

$$t=6,188[min]*\frac{1}{60}\left[\frac{hr}{min}\right]*\frac{1}{24}\left[\frac{day}{hr}\right] \leftarrow eq.5$$

Eq.5 converts the time from minutes to days.

$$t=4.30[days]$$

Answer: C

Solution #37

Find: $\tau_{max,B}$ ← the maximum shear stress in the beam at point B.

Given:

$P_C=8[k]$ ← the point load at point C.

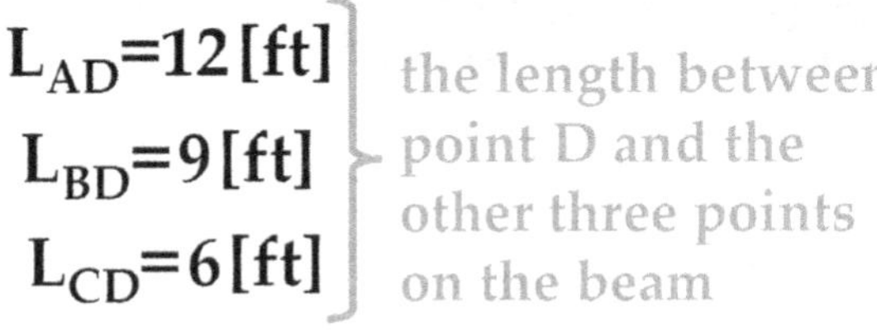

$L_{AD}=12[ft]$

$L_{BD}=9[ft]$

$L_{CD}=6[ft]$

the length between point D and the other three points on the beam

$b_w=4[in]$ ← the beam width

$b_h=5[in]$ ← the beam height

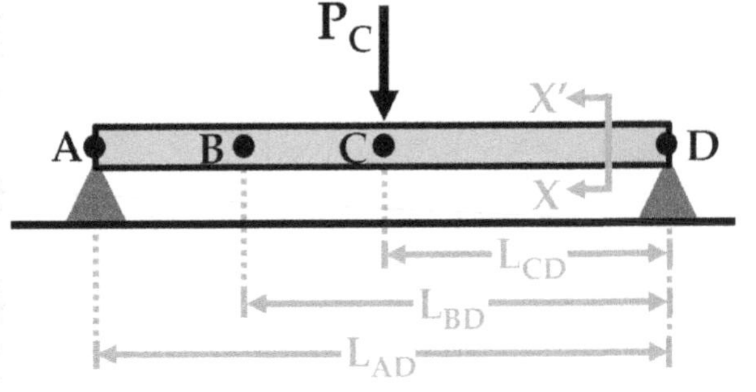

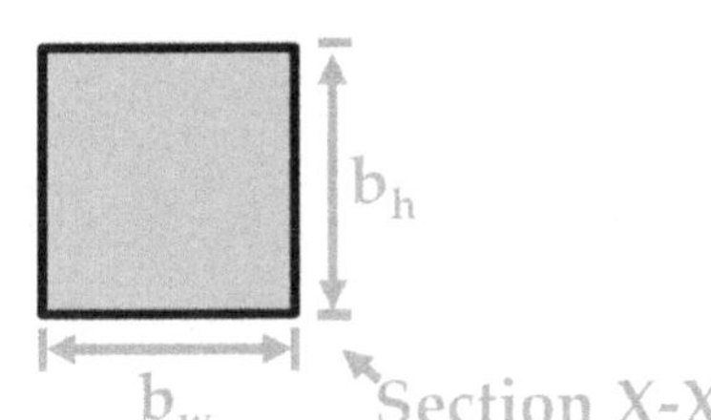

A) 0.3[ksi]

B) 0.4[ksi]

C) 4[ksi]

D) 40[ksi]

Analysis:

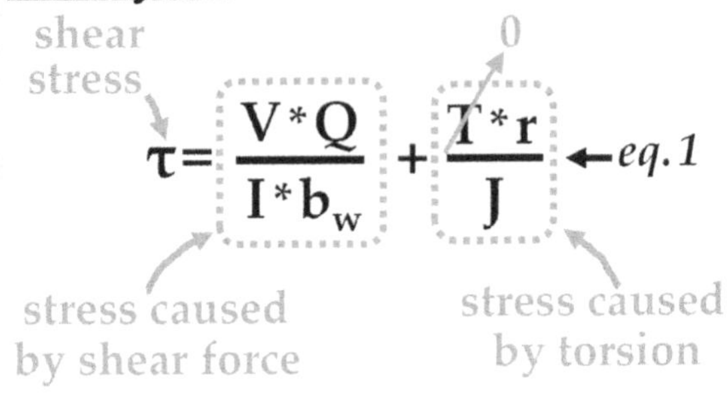

$$\tau=\frac{V*Q}{I*b_w}+\frac{T*r}{J} \quad \leftarrow eq.1$$

Eq.1 computes the shear stress in the beam caused by shear force and torsion.

Since there is no torsional force acting on the beam, the second term of eq.1 cancels out.

shear force at point B; maximum statical moment of the area; area moment of inertia; beam width

$$\tau_{max,B}=\frac{V_B*Q_{max}}{I*b_w} \quad \leftarrow eq.2$$

Eq.1 reduces down to eq.2.

In eq. 2, we added the subscripts 'B' and 'max', referring to point B and the maximum values of the statical moment and shear stress.

$b_w=4[in]$ $b_h=5[in]$

$$I=\frac{b_w*b_h^3}{12} \quad \leftarrow eq.3$$

Eq.3 computes the area moment of inertia for a rectangle.

$$I=\frac{4[in]*(5[in])^3}{12}$$

Plug in variables b_w and b_h into eq.3, then solve for I.

$$I=41.67[in^4]$$

Solution #37 (cont.)

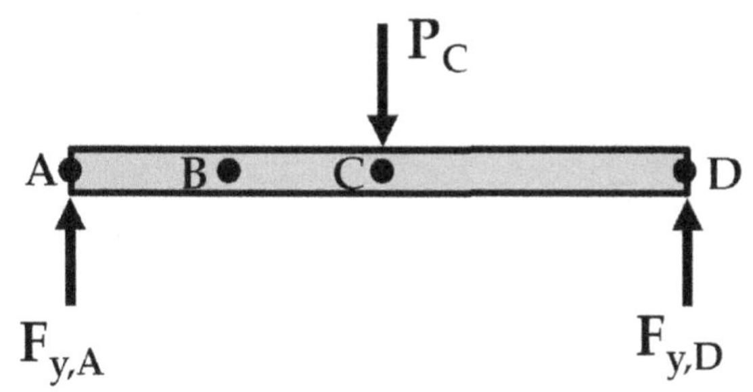

Figure 1

Figure 1 shows the point load at point C and the vertical reaction forces at points A and D.

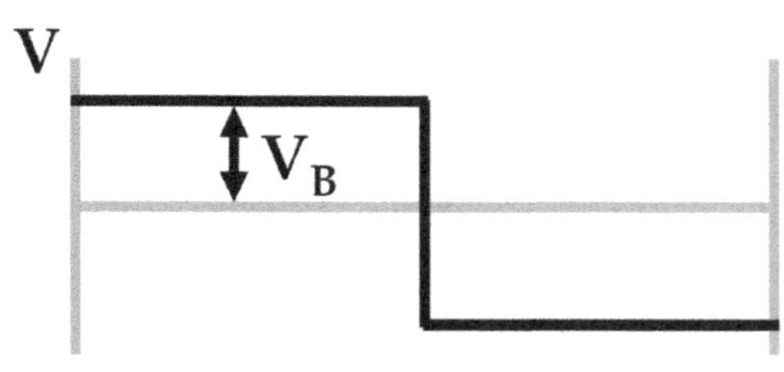

Figure 2

Figure 2 shows the shear force acting along the length of the beam.

From Figures 1 and 2, we notice the shear force at point B equals the reaction force at point A.

$$F_{y,A}=V_B$$

To find the shear force at point B, V_B, use eq.4 to compute the vertical reaction force point A, $F_{y,A}$.

$$\Sigma M_D=0=-F_{y,A}*L_{AD}+P_C*L_{CD} \leftarrow eq.4$$

Solve eq.4 for $F_{y,A}$.

$P_C=8[k]$ $L_{CD}=6[ft]$

$$F_{y,A}=\frac{P_C*L_{CD}}{L_{AD}} \leftarrow eq.5$$

$F_{y,A}=V_B$ $L_{AD}=12[ft]$

Plug in variables $F_{y,A}$, P_C, L_{CD} and L_{AD} into eq.5, then solve for V_B.

$$V_B=\frac{8[k]*6[ft]}{12[ft]}$$

$$V_B=4[k]$$

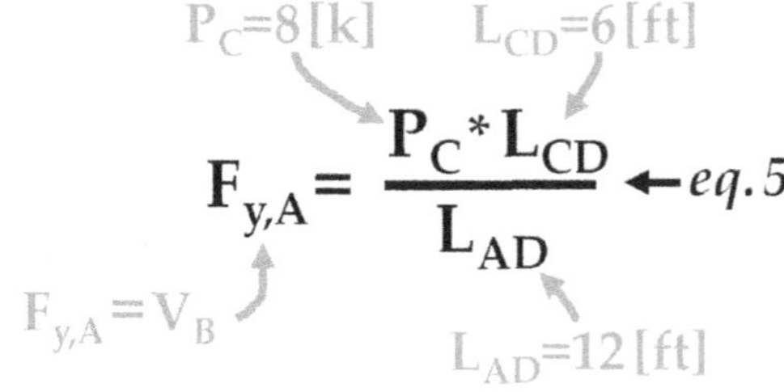

distance area

$$Q_{max}=y*A \leftarrow eq.6$$

The maximum statical moment of area occurs at a point which maximizes the product of the distance y and the area A.

Solution #37 (cont.)

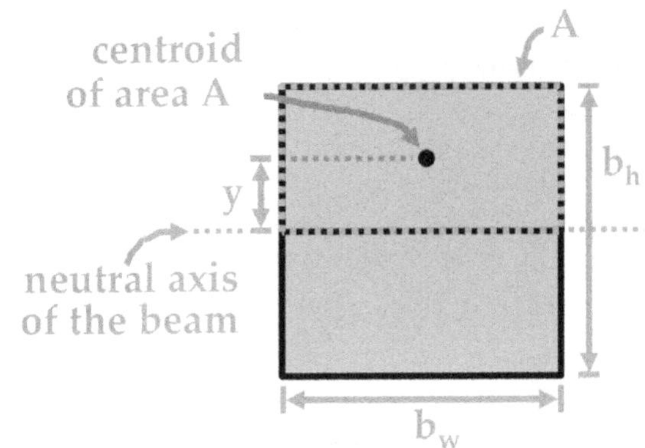

Figure 3

For eq.6, let the area A equal the area of the top half of the beam.

In eq.6, let the distance y equal the distance between the centroid of area A and the neutral axis of the entire beam.

b_w=4[in] b_h=5[in]

$$A=b_w*(0.5*b_h) \leftarrow eq.7$$

Plug in variables b_w and b_h into eq.7, then solve for A.

$$A=4[in]*(0.5*5[in])$$

$$A=10[in^2]$$

Plug in variable b_h into eq.8, then solve for y.

b_h=5[in]

$$y=0.5*b_h-(0.5*0.5*b_h) \leftarrow eq.8$$

$$y=0.5*5[in]-(0.5*0.5*5[in])$$

$$y=1.25[in]$$

y=1.25[in] A=10[in^2]

$$Q_{max}=y*A \leftarrow eq.6$$

Plug in variable y and A into eq.6, then solve for Q_{max}.

$$Q_{max}=1.25[in]*10[in^2]$$

$$Q_{max}=12.5[in^3]$$

Solution #37 (cont.)

$V_B=4\,[k]$, $Q_{max}=12.5\,[in^3]$, $I=41.67\,[in^4]$, $b_w=4\,[in]$

$$\tau_{max,B}=\frac{V_B * Q_{max}}{I * b_w} \leftarrow eq. 2$$

Plug in variables V_B, Q_{max}, I and b_w into eq. 2, then solve for the maximum shear stress at point B.

$$\tau_{max,B}=\frac{4\,[k] * 12.5\,[in^3]}{41.67\,[in^4] * 4\,[in]}$$

$$\tau_{max,B}=0.30\,[k/in^2]$$

Answer: A

Solution #38

Find: H_B ← the height of the soil when loaded at 16,000 [lb/ft²]

Given:

H_A=1.000[in] ← height of the sample when loaded at $\sigma_{v,A}$

ID	σ'_v[lb/ft²] (vertical effective stress)	e (void ratio)
A	8,000	1.000
B	16,000	0.914

the clay soil is normally consolidated at $\sigma_{v,A}$=8,000[lb/ft²]

A) 0.828[in]
B) 0.914[in]
C) 0.957[in]
D) 1.000[in]

Analysis:

$$H_B=H_A-\sigma_c \leftarrow eq.1$$

height of sample at loadings B and A (H_B, H_A); primary consolidation which occurs between loading A and loading B (σ_c)

Eq.1 computes the height of the clay sample for loading B.

$$\sigma_c=\left(\frac{H_o*C_c}{1+e_o}\right)*\log\left(\frac{\sigma'_{vo}+\Delta\sigma'_v}{\sigma'_v}\right) \leftarrow eq.2$$

initial height (H_o); compression index (C_c); additional vertical effective stress ($\Delta\sigma'_v$); primary consolidation (σ_c); initial void ratio (e_o); initial vertical effective stress

Eq.2 computes the primary consolidation of the sample.

Loading A is considered the initial condition.

$$H_o=H_A=1.000[in]$$

The initial height of the soil is the height of the soil for loading A.

$$e_o=e_A=1.000$$

The initial void ratio of the soil is the void ratio at loading A.

$$\sigma'_{vo}=\sigma'_{v,A}=8,000[lb/ft^2]$$

The initial vertical effective stress corresponds to loading A.

$$\Delta\sigma'_v=\sigma'_{v,B}-\sigma'_{v,A} \leftarrow eq.3$$

$\sigma'_{v,A}$=8,000[lb/ft²]; $\sigma'_{v,B}$=16,000[lb/ft²]

The additional vertical effective stress is the difference in stress between loading A and loading B.

Solution #38 (cont.)

$$\Delta\sigma_v = 16{,}000\,[lb/ft^2] - 8{,}000\,[lb/ft^2]$$

$$\Delta\sigma'_v = 8{,}000\,[lb/ft^2]$$

$e_A = 1.000$ $e_B = 0.914$

$$C_c = \frac{e_A - e_B}{\log(\sigma'_{o,B}/\sigma'_{o,A})} \leftarrow eq.4$$

$\sigma_{o,B} = 16{,}000\,[lb/ft^2]$ $\sigma_{o,A} = 8{,}000\,[lb/ft^2]$

Eq.4 computes the compression index of the clay sample

Plug in variables e_A, e_B, $\sigma_{o,B}$ and $\sigma_{o,A}$ into eq.4, then solve for C_c.

$$C_c = \frac{1.000 - 0.914}{\log(16{,}000\,[lb/ft^2]/8{,}000\,[lb/ft^2])}$$

$$C_c = 0.286$$

Drop the units from the compression index calculation.

$H_o = 1.000\,[in]$ $C_c = 0.286$ $\Delta\sigma'_v = 8{,}000\,[lb/ft^2]$

$$\sigma_c = \left(\frac{H_o * C_c}{1 + e_o}\right) * \log\left(\frac{\sigma'_{vo} + \Delta\sigma'_v}{\sigma'_{vo}}\right) \leftarrow eq.2$$

$e_o = 1.000$ $\sigma'_{vo} = 8{,}000\,[lb/ft^2]$

Plug the known variables into the right hand side of eq.2, then solve for the primary consolidation, σ_c.

$$\sigma_c = \left(\frac{1.000\,[in] * 0.286}{1 + 1.000}\right) * \log\left(\frac{8{,}000\,[lb/ft^2] + 8{,}000\,[lb/ft^2]}{8{,}000\,[lb/ft^2]}\right)$$

$$\sigma_c = 0.043\,[in]$$

$H_A = 1.000\,[in]$ $\sigma_c = 0.043\,[in]$

$$H_B = H_A - \sigma_c \leftarrow eq.1$$

Plug in variables H_A and σ_c into eq.1, then solve for H_B.

$$H_B = 1.000\,[in] - 0.043\,[in]$$

$$H_B = 0.957\,[in]$$

Answer: C

Solution #39

Find: R ← the rate of grade change along the crest vertical curve

Given:

$g_1=1.5\%$ ← approach grade

$g_2=-2.5\%$ ← departing grade

$a_y=-0.02*g$ ← vertical acceleration experienced by car passengers while driving over the curve

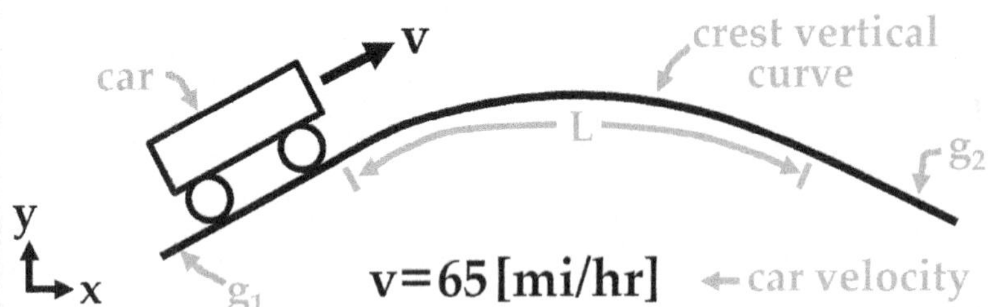

$v=65\,[mi/hr]$ ← car velocity

A) $-9.4*10^{-4}[\%/ft]$

B) $-3.8*10^{-3}[\%/ft]$

C) $-7.1*10^{-3}[\%/ft]$

D) $-2.6*10^{-2}[\%/ft]$

Analysis:

$$R=\frac{g_2-g_1}{L} \quad \leftarrow eq.1$$

(R: rate of grade change; g_2: departing grade; g_1: approach grade; L: curve length)

Eq.1 computes the rate of grade change for a vertical curve.

$$a_y=\frac{dv_y}{dt} \quad \leftarrow eq.2$$

(a_y: vertical acceleration; dv_y: change in vertical velocity; dt: change in time)

Eq.2 computes the vertical acceleration of the car due to driving over the vertical curve.

$$L=v*dt \quad \leftarrow eq.3$$

(L: curve length; v: car velocity)

Assuming it takes the car a duration of dt to drive the length of the vertical curve, eq.3 computes the length of the curve,

$$dt=L/v \quad \leftarrow eq.4$$

Solve eq.3 for dt.

$$a_y=\frac{dv_y}{dt} \quad \leftarrow eq.2$$

(dt = L/v)

Plug in L/v for dt into eq.2, then solve for L.

$$a_y=\frac{dv_y}{L/v}$$

Solution #39 (cont.)

$$L=\frac{dv_y * v}{a_y} \leftarrow eq.5$$

$$a_y=-0.02 * g \leftarrow eq.6$$

g=32.2 [ft/s²]

Eq.6 computes the vertical acceleration due to driving over the vertical curve.

$$a_y=-0.02 * 32.2[ft/s^2]$$

Plug in the vertical acceleration term into eq.6, then solve for a_y.

$$a_y=-0.644[ft/s^2]$$

$$dv_y=v_{y,2}-v_{y,1} \leftarrow eq.7$$

$v_{y,2}$: vertical velocity on the departing grade

$v_{y,1}$: vertical velocity on the approach grade

Eq.7 computes the change in velocity of the car in the vertical direction before and after the curve.

$$v_{y,2}=v * g_2 \leftarrow eq.8$$

v: car velocity; g_2: departing grade

Eq.8 computes the vertical velocity of the car on the departing grade.

$$v=65\left[\frac{mi}{hr}\right] * 5{,}280\left[\frac{ft}{mi}\right] * \frac{1}{60}\left[\frac{hr}{min}\right] * \frac{1}{60}\left[\frac{min}{s}\right] \leftarrow eq.9$$

$$v=95.33[ft/s]$$

Eq.9 converts the velocity to units of feet per second.

$$v_{y,2}=v * g_2 \leftarrow eq.8$$

$v=95.33[ft/s]$

$g_2=-2.5\%=-0.025$

Plug in variables v and g_2 into eq.8, then solve for $v_{y,2}$.

$$v_{y,2}=95.33[ft/s] * (-0.025)$$

$$v_{y,2}=-2.38[ft/s]$$

Solution #39 (cont.)

$v=95.33\,[ft/s]$

$$v_{y,1}=v*g_1 \quad \leftarrow eq.10$$

$g_1=1.5\%=0.015$

Plug in variables v and g_1 into eq.10, then solve for $v_{y,1}$.

$$v_{y,1}=95.33\,[ft/s]*0.015$$

$$v_{y,1}=1.43\,[ft/s]$$

$v_{y,2}=-2.38\,[ft/s]$ $v_{y,1}=1.43\,[ft/s]$

$$dv_y=v_{y,2}-v_{y,1} \quad \leftarrow eq.7$$

Plug in variables $v_{y,1}$, and $v_{y,2}$, into eq.7, then solve for dv_y.

$$dv_y=-2.38\,[ft/s]-1.43\,[ft/s]$$

$$dv_y=-3.81\,[ft/s]$$

$dv_y=-3.81[ft/s]$ $v=95.33\,[ft/s]$

$$L=\frac{dv_y*v}{a_y} \quad \leftarrow eq.5$$

$a_y=-0.644\,[ft/s^2]$

Plug in variables dv_y, v and a_y into eq.5, then solve for the length of the vertical curve, L.

$$L=\frac{-3.81\,[ft/s]*95.33[ft/s]}{-0.644\,[ft/s^2]}$$

$$L=564.0[ft]$$

$g_2=-0.025$ $g_1=0.015$

$$R=\frac{g_2-g_1}{L} \quad \leftarrow eq.1$$

$L=564.0\,[ft]$

Plug in variables g_2, g_1 and L into eq.1, then solve for the rate of grade change, R.

Solution #39 (cont.)

$$R = \frac{-0.025 - 0.015}{564.0[ft]}$$

$$R = -7.092 * 10^{-5}[ft^{-1}] * 100\% \leftarrow eq.\ 11$$

Eq. 11 converts the rate of grade change from decimals per foot to percent per foot.

$$R = -7.092 * 10^{-3}[\%/ft]$$

Answer: C

Solution #40

Find: The point with the lowest pressure.

Given:

Fluid	Density
water	998[kg/m³]
ethane	570[kg/m³]
kerosene	820[kg/m³]
benzene	874[kg/m³]

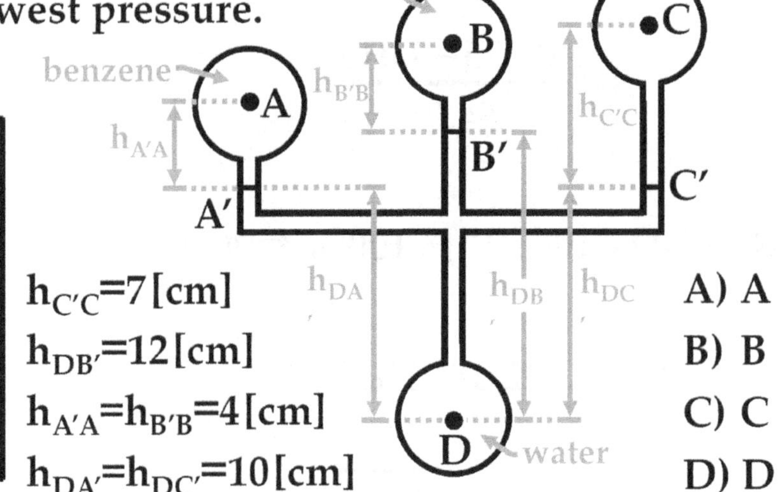

$h_{C'C}$=7[cm]
$h_{DB'}$=12[cm]
$h_{A'A}$=$h_{B'B}$=4[cm]
$h_{DA'}$=$h_{DC'}$=10[cm]

A) A
B) B
C) C
D) D

Analysis:

CASE I: if $\Delta P_{AD} > \Delta P_{BD}$ and $\Delta P_{AD} > \Delta P_{CD}$ → A

CASE II: if $\Delta P_{BD} > \Delta P_{AD}$ and $\Delta P_{BD} > \Delta P_{CD}$ → B

CASE III: if $\Delta P_{CD} > \Delta P_{AD}$ and $\Delta P_{CD} > \Delta P_{BD}$ → C

point having the lowest pressure?

Using point D as a reference, the point with the lowest pressure will experience the largest change in pressure from point D to that point

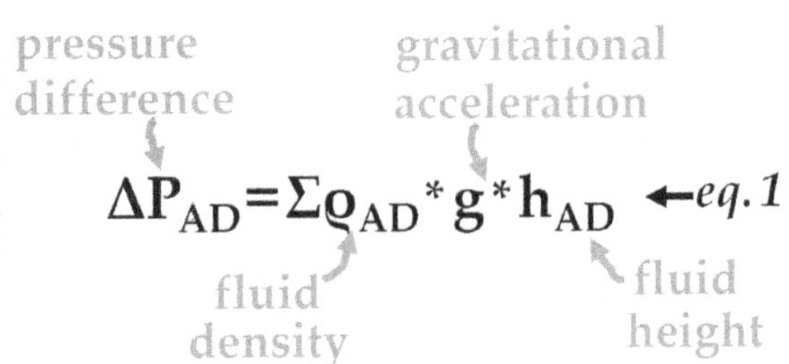

$$\Delta P_{AD} = \Sigma \rho_{AD} * g * h_{AD} \quad \leftarrow eq.1$$

Eq.1 computes the pressure difference between points A and D.

$$\Delta P_{AD} = g * (\rho_w * h_{DA'} + \rho_b * h_{A'A}) \quad \leftarrow eq.2$$

water, benzene

Write out the summation in eq.1.

In eq.2, subscript "w" refers to water and subscript "b" refers to benzene.

given heights; conversion factor

$$\left.\begin{aligned} h_{C'C} &= 7[cm] \\ h_{DB'} &= 12[cm] \\ h_{A'A} = h_{B'B} &= 4[cm] \\ h_{DA'} = h_{DC'} &= 10[cm] \end{aligned}\right\} * \frac{1}{100}\left[\frac{m}{cm}\right] = \begin{aligned} h_{C'C} &= 0.07[m] \\ h_{DB'} &= 0.12[m] \\ h_{A'A} = h_{B'B} &= 0.04[m] \\ h_{DA'} = h_{DC'} &= 0.10[m] \end{aligned}$$

Convert the given height values to units of meters.

Solution #40 (cont.)

$h_{DA'}=0.10\,[m]$ $\quad h_{A'A}=0.04\,[m]$

$$\Delta P_{AD}=g*(\varrho_w*h_{DA'}+\varrho_b*h_{A'A}) \leftarrow eq.2$$

$g=9.81\,[m/s^2]$ $\quad \varrho_b=874\,[kg/m^3]$ $\quad \varrho_w=998\,[kg/m^3]$

Plug in variables g, ϱ_w, $h_{DA'}$, ϱ_b and $h_{A'A}$ into eq.2, then solve for ΔP_{AD}.

$$\Delta P_{AD}=9.81[m/s^2]*(998[kg/m^3]*0.10[m]+874[kg/m^3]*0.04[m])$$

$$\Delta P_{AD}=1{,}322\left[\frac{kg}{m*s^2}\right]*1\left[\frac{Pa*m*s^2}{kg}\right]=1{,}322[Pa]$$

Convert the pressure to units of Pascals.

$h_{DB'}=0.12\,[m]$ $\quad h_{B'B}=0.04\,[m]$

$$\Delta P_{BD}=g*(\varrho_w*h_{DB'}+\varrho_k*h_{B'B}) \leftarrow eq.3$$

$g=9.81\,[m/s^2]$ $\quad \varrho_k=820\,[kg/m^3]$ $\quad \varrho_w=998\,[kg/m^3]$

Eq.3 computes the pressure difference between points B and D.

$$\Delta P_{BD}=9.81[m/s^2]*(998[kg/m^3]*0.12[m]+820[kg/m^3]*0.04[m])$$

$$\Delta P_{BD}=1{,}497\left[\frac{kg}{m*s^2}\right]*1\left[\frac{Pa*m*s^2}{kg}\right]=1{,}497[Pa]$$

Convert the pressure to units of Pascals.

$h_{DC'}=0.10\,[m]$ $\quad h_{C'C}=0.07\,[m]$

$$\Delta P_{CD}=g*(\varrho_w*h_{DC'}+\varrho_e*h_{C'C}) \leftarrow eq.4$$

$g=9.81\,[m/s^2]$ $\quad \varrho_e=570\,[kg/m^3]$ $\quad \varrho_w=998\,[kg/m^3]$

Eq.4 computes the pressure difference between points C and D.

$$\Delta P_{BD}=9.81[m/s^2]*(998[kg/m^3]*0.10[m]+570[kg/m^3]*0.07[m])$$

$$\Delta P_{BD}=1{,}370\left[\frac{kg}{m*s^2}\right]*1\left[\frac{Pa*m*s^2}{kg}\right]=1{,}370[Pa]$$

Convert the pressure to units of Pascals.

Answer: B

ΔP_{BD} is the largest of the three pressure differences.

(page intentionally left blank)

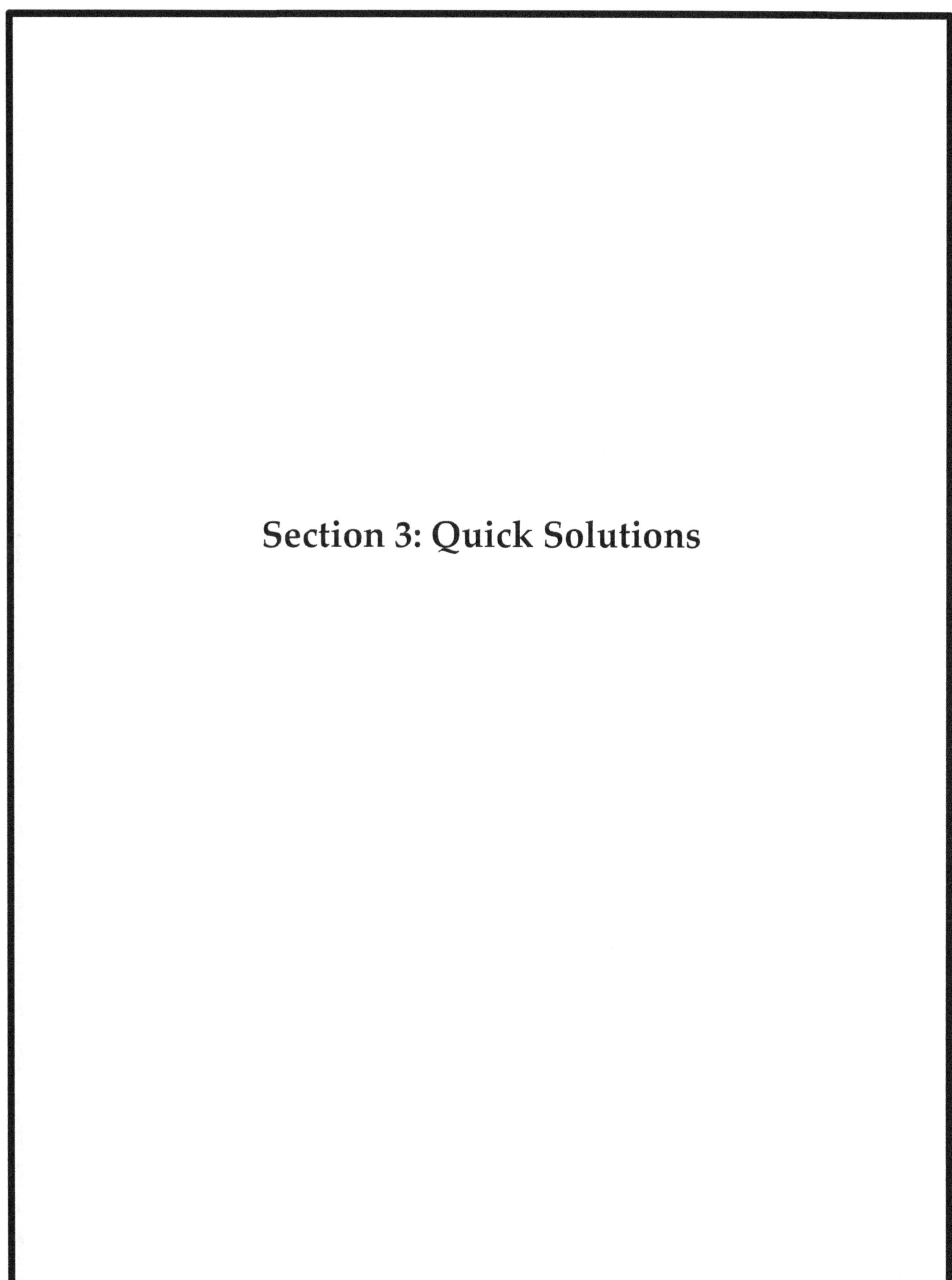

Section 3: Quick Solutions

(page intentionally left blank)

1. D
2. B
3. D
4. B
5. D
6. D
7. D
8. B
9. B
10. A
11. A
12. A
13. C
14. B
15. D
16. C
17. D
18. C
19. C
20. D

21. D
22. C
23. C
24. A
25. A
26. B
27. A
28. B
29. B
30. D
31. B
32. A
33. B
34. A
35. A
36. C
37. A
38. C
39. C
40. B

Notes:

Notes:

Made in the USA
Monee, IL
07 September 2023